MY TURKEY HAS HYPOTHERMIA, OFFICER

A True Crime Memoir

Stories of humor, tragedy and inspiration from my life
as a police officer in Alaska

By
Peyton Merideth

2

ISBN: 978-1-57833-778-1

My Turkey Has Hypothermia, Officer

Book Design: Carmen Maldonado, Todd Communications
The typeface for this book was set in Calibri 11.5.
Printed in China through **Alaska Print Brokers**, Anchorage, Alaska
First printing July 2021

Published by:

Gray Ghost Publishing Co.

Distributed by:

Todd Communications
611 E. 12th Ave. • Anchorage, Alaska 99501-4603
(907) 274-TODD (8633) • Fax: (907) 929-5550
with other offices in Juneau and Fairbanks, Alaska
sales@toddcom.com • WWW.ALASKABOOKSANDCALENDARS.COM

To Kristi

Being married to a cop isn't easy. Thank you for sharing your life with me and remaining by my side during this adventure.

I have told the stories in this book as accurately as I can from memory. Some of the names have been changed. Any changed names that resemble the names of real people are purely coincidental.

TABLE OF CONTENTS

INTRODUCTION

It's the decomposing corpse of someone you have never met and yet will never forget for the rest of your life that's truly unforgettable. You see, it wasn't the first dead body I ever saw that I will never forget—it was the first dead body I smelled. It's funny, and a bit ironic I guess, how someone's final journey above ground can affect your life, a stranger's life, in so many ways. Allow me to explain.

It was May 1999 and it was hot. I'm not talking Tennessee-in-August hot, but eighty degrees is downright sweltering for Interior Alaska in May. I was working patrol in North Pole (yes that North Pole where the city streets are lined with light poles that look like candy canes, and the Santa Claus House is the most popular tourist attraction in town). Forgive my need to specify, but whenever I mention North Pole, people tend to think of *The* North Pole, not the city of North Pole, Alaska. Incorporated on January 15, 1953 and with just over 2,000 residents, North Pole, Alaska can be found about 15 miles South of Fairbanks along the Richardson Highway. It is also about 120 miles South of the Arctic Circle, so not hardly at the top of the world as its name sake would imply.

Anyway, I was dispatched to the residence of a "concerned and annoyed" neighbor. "Concerned" because they were tired of the foul stench drifting out of their neighbor's house and "annoyed" because they could not complain to their neighbor personally. It turned out they had not seen their neighbor, a middle-aged guy, coming or going from the home for about three weeks. Three of the hottest weeks on record.

If this was baseball, that would be strike one *and* strike two.

I had only been on the job for a month, and I was still riding with my training officer, Mark. So while I wasn't a total rookie, and I'd seen a fair share of things already, I knew there was a lot left for me to experience still. Mark was, and still is, a beast of a man with the ability to change from human battering ram to teddy bear. He started his career policing in the Aleutian Island fishing community of Sand Point before working in the South Central coastal community of Yakutat. Originally from Delta, Mark moved back to interior Alaska to live and work closer to his family.

Knocking on the door was a formality at this point. Flies buzzed against both the inside and outside of the picture window.

Strike three, you're out.

The door was locked, but that's nothing a size 12 shoe can't handle. In we went, and then the curve ball hit.

While in the academy, I had been told that a rotting human doesn't smell like an animal or spoiled food in the fridge or any other putrid smell you can imagine. It had its own smell, one that couldn't be described, but many instructors tried. When that door opened, the smell literally about knocked me over. When that odor wound its way up my nose, I threw up in my mouth...and that smelled better.

We found the guy in the garage. He was sitting in his car with a beer bottle upside down in his lap and another empty bottle in the drink holder. His termination letter from work was lying on the passenger seat. The keys were in the ignition, which was turned on, but the car had long ago run out of gas.

Since I've already used a baseball analogy, I'll just run with another: for my first death investigation I hit one right out of the park.

This guy, who in "real life" was of average build, had turned as green as Kermit the Frog and bloated to a size I refer to as "Biggest Loser Big." We really pissed off the neighbors when we opened the garage door, but they weren't the ones standing in a hundred-degree garage with a dead guy getting stinkier by the minute, and he wasn't getting any less dead.

In retrospect, it was not difficult to determine how or why this guy had decided to permanently reside on the wrong side of the dirt. I like easy, and this case was easy. It was suicide by carbon monoxide poisoning.

After spending a couple hours with my new green friend, the van from the funeral home arrived to haul him away. There were two guys working that day. One was a seasoned...well...funeral home technician, I guess you would call him. The other guy was, no kidding, working his first day on the job.

If I thought I had hit a home run, hell, this guy just pitched a perfect game in the World Series. At least it wasn't *my* first day! Of course I'm already thinking, "Hey, sucks to be you, this is your problem now. I go from point A to point B...got nothing to do with C." The dead guy was on him now.

The new guy walks into the garage, looks at the stinky green guy and walks right back out. On his way to the van, I barely make out a faint, "Fuck you, I quit."

And suddenly, I learned what "low man on the totem pole" really meant.

The remaining funeral home worker glanced at Mark and me, then turned to me and gave me a piece of advice with this instruction: "You take his legs and I'll get his arms. Just don't let him *spill*."

I couldn't resist asking, "What exactly is going to spill?"

He pointed to the car where our bloated green friend sat behind the wheel on his final drive. "Him."

I got his left leg out without any problem, but his right heel, and I mean the very heel end of his tennis shoe caught on the door jam and damned if this stinky guy didn't spill. His crotch split open, and out the bottom of his pants poured the entire contents of his abdominal cavity. My boots were covered in slime, and what didn't land on my boots splashed onto my pants. I felt like Andy Dufresne crawling through the sewer tunnel in the **Shawshank Redemption**, and I guarantee I smelled worse!

After Mark pulled himself up off the ground from laughing, all he could say was, "Sucks to be you, Peyton! Aren't you glad you became a cop?"

Twenty years later...yeah, I am.

I was born on September 3, 1977 in Memphis, Tennessee. My mom and dad were school teachers. Working for the Memphis City School District in the 1970s was frustrating and difficult. Racial tensions were high in the South and Memphis was rapidly expanding. At the time, my mom's sister and her husband were stationed at

Fort Wainwright, Alaska, an Army base just outside Fairbanks. One summer visit to the Last Frontier when I was three was all it took, and my parents fell in love with Alaska. They wasted no time, and a week after my fourth birthday, we moved to Fairbanks.

I would like to think I was a good kid. Yes, I might have quickly departed a house party when the police showed up. Yes, I might have done a couple keg stands or two. But I never crossed the line. I graduated from Lathrop High School in 1995, eager to move down south for college. Warm weather, no snow, and co-ed dorms. What could possibly go wrong?

But like many of my friends, I stayed in Fairbanks because of a girl. Since I could say my first piece of advice to you is to be more careful when moving a dead body, let my second piece of advice be this: please encourage your kids not to stick around their hometown for college because of a high school romance. Of course, my relationship didn't last, but by the time it ended, I was a quarter of the way through my course studies in criminal justice at the University of Alaska Fairbanks. I decided to stay in Fairbanks and finish my degree. And that shaped my future in a very real way.

In 1998 two significant events occurred in my life. First, I graduated from college. For those of you who just scrolled up a paragraph, yes, I said I finished high school in 1995. Getting your bachelor's degree in criminal justice is not rocket science, thank goodness, so I was able to make it through college in a little over three years. Second, I attended the Interior Alaska Police Academy which was put on by the Fairbanks Police Department.

The previous winter two Fairbanks officers had broken their legs in separate snow machine accidents. Since they were already on light duty, the city decided to put them in charge of an academy and charge $5,000 for students to attend. That was a lot of money for me back then—so much that I kept the cashed check as a souvenir. But it was worth every penny. And since the academy was scheduled during the summer, I didn't have to worry about missing school and I could graduate on time.

Being accepted into the program came with some caveats. Namely, that meant a background check... Yeah, so remember those high school parties and other shenanigans? Suddenly, I did too. The officer in charge happened to be the same officer I ran from after a high school fight in the snow dump behind my high school. The detective who did my background investigation? Yeah, I used to do keg stands at his house when he and his wife left their teenage daughter home alone during an adult-only vacation. Later, I would work with that officer for fifteen years. And the detective, well, he accused me of stealing presents from under his Christmas tree. (I didn't.)

Now, I always knew I wanted to be a police officer. And in the twilight of my career, I still love law enforcement, but I would be lying if I said that I didn't see the world through different eyes than those of a twenty-one-year-old, naïve, rookie cop ready to take on the world.

In 2000, I left the North Pole Police Department (NPPD) and was hired on with the Fairbanks Police Department (FPD). I was promoted to detective and spent thirteen years investigating major crimes. Every time I thought I had seen it all, something new reaffirmed that humans are capable of doing horrible things to one another. However, despite the daily evils I witnessed, I still find satisfaction in knowing that, every so often, I made a difference that changed someone's life for the better or gave a family a sense of closure after the death of a loved one. You take the good with the bad, and I can live with that. I always tell my dad, the consummate worrier, "Someone has to do the job; it might as well be me."

From all my years of experience, I've learned this: there are two fundamental essentials for any police officer if they want to make it to retirement alive, happy, and still married. First, marry an understanding and loving person who is willing to listen to every horrible detail about your day when you make it home at the end of your shift. Communication is a fundamental key to any marriage, and this is magnified when you are married to a cop. After all, how many dozens of child pornography videos did you have to watch today? How many dead bodies spilled on you today? How many people got in your face and cussed you out? Police officers are human, not robots without feelings, and they need to talk to someone about these things.

Second, you must have a hobby or a distraction that takes you away from police work and occupies your mind with something enjoyable that has nothing to do with the job. For me, that distraction is hunting and music. I love singing, been doing it all my life. I used to run through the house naked carrying a guitar singing "Look at my beautiful body." Hunting is my passion and my way of escaping the stressful world of police work. I've shared hunting adventures with friends and family all over Alaska and enjoyed several safaris in South Africa. The interior décor of our house resembles a natural history museum. Every mounted trophy represents a memory, a fun adventure I can reflect on when times are tough. Some of these pieces of art represent hunts done in honor of fallen officers. More on that later.

But with all the evil that we see, why do we choose to be police officers? Let me tell you one more story before I end this little introduction. Once case stands out to me where a father filed a police report stating his thirteen-year-old daughter was having sex with the father's thirty-something-year-old best friend. Nice right? Trust me; it's more common than you think.

I brought the girl in for an interview, and of course, she was "in love with him," and she didn't want to get him in trouble. I've heard the same song and dance a thousand times. There is no one in this world more frustrating to deal with than a teenage girl with an attitude. By all accounts, she was a bright girl, did well in school, but to me she didn't seem truly happy. She seemed downtrodden and depressed. The look in her eye told me she knew what was happening was wrong, and she eventually admitted to the affair. The cost of the admission was that she hated me because she knew I was going to put "her man" in prison.

To make a long story short, we wired up the dad and facilitated a meeting between him and his "best friend" in a sandwich shop. The suspect admitted to the dad he was having sex with his daughter, but that he was only teaching her how to "do it right" so she would not be hurt by someone else who didn't care so much about her. Caring guy, right? The background music playing in the restaurant was Taylor Swift's "When You are Fifteen." Pure poetic justice.

Three years later, I was leaving a local high school after teaching a forensics class. Someone tugged on the back of my jacket, and I turned around. It was the same girl and although I couldn't recall her name right away, I immediately recognized her face. She looked beautiful, especially with an ear-to-ear grin. We embraced for a long hug. When she stepped back, her eyes were filled with tears. But through them, she stared me right in the eye, apologized and then thanked me for changing her life. She told me she understood what had happened was wrong, and that I was right. When a tear rolled down her cheek, I about lost it.

That is why we are police officers.

I wrote this book primarily for my family, to document my professional life so that one day my children will understand the trials and tribulations that police officers routinely face. And I want my children to know what their dad experienced in his lifetime. As of this writing, Peyton, my oldest boy is set on becoming an Alaska State Wildlife Trooper. Hunter, who more so than our other children just wants to be like his dad in so many ways, wants to be a municipal police officer wherever we call home in retirement. Our twins, Asher and Taylor are nine, and still imagining their futures, and our newest edition, Presley, is just a month old at the time of this writing. She was an unplanned blessing; one we are so very thankful for.

If there is one thing being a cop will teach you, it's not to let the little things get in the way of enjoying the people in your life. Two students in my graduating academy class have died. One committed suicide and the other had an undiagnosed heart condition which caused him to die in his sleep. Whenever I speak at academy commencement ceremonies, I always make it a point to tell the graduates to cherish the time they spent together because people often die before we have a chance to say goodbye. And in some roundabout way, that reflection has led me to my reasons for writing these words down today.

When I set out to write this book, the one thing I promised myself was that I would not embellish anything. I want to be as upfront and honest as I can because I think that is exactly what the reader deserves. Want to know what it's like to be a police officer or detective? Well, I'll tell you, and I won't hold back. Brutal honesty is what I offer you. Oh, that and I really, really don't want to be sued for libel. For that reason, I have either omitted or changed some of the names mentioned here. For brevity, some of the interviews referenced throughout have been paraphrased, but the context and tone remain the same as I remember them.

In December of 2019, I retired from police work in Alaska after spending nearly twenty-one years serving the citizens of Interior Alaska. With our oldest children moving Outside for college, we made the decision to spend the next chapter of our lives in the Treasure Valley of Southwestern Idaho. Although I miss the extraordinary hunting opportunities in Alaska, I sure don't miss the bitter cold and shoveling snow. I've continued my career in Boise working as an investigator with the Ada County Prosecutor's Office. It's still police work, albeit at a much slower and stress-free pace.

As a man, a father, and a police officer of twenty-plus years and despite all I've seen and experienced, I still trust that most people are inherently good and want to do the right thing by their fellow man. But there are those that don't. And when the line between good and evil is crossed, there are men and women on the street who are entrusted to protect the rights scripted for all people by our founding fathers and bestowed upon us by our Heavenly Father. Though there are thousands of stories that should be and need to be told, the stories told in these pages are mine.

CHAPTER 1
FUN TIMES

The Richardson Highway runs about 368 miles and connects Fairbanks to Valdez, a major fishing hub at the head of Prince William Sound. I can't count the hours I've spent on that highway working innumerable motor vehicle accidents. During the winter, the icy roads cause hundreds of fender benders that keep tow trucks busy pulling vehicles from the deep, snowy ditches on both sides of the highway. During the summer, when drivers inevitably speed up, the accidents often turn deadly.

So, it was on a sunny Saturday, not long after being promoted to sergeant in 2018, that I found myself running radar out on the highway. We didn't have a traffic ticket quota, but I always liked running traffic to stay busy, and I quite frankly was trying to be a good leader and inspire my troops to be proactive. If the sergeant made time to stroke a few tickets, they could too.

That day I pulled over a blue minivan for going seventy-five in a sixty. Not the end of the world, but well over my ten-over threshold. I recall there being heavy traffic at the time, so for my safety I approached the vehicle on the passenger side. The driver, a heavy set woman wearing what looked like surgical scrubs, rolled down the passenger window.

Most of the time I was polite on traffic stops until it was time not to be nice. I always subscribed to the Dalton theory from the movie *Road House* (you millennials will have no idea what I'm talking about).

"Good morning, I'm Sergeant Merideth with the Fairbanks Police Department. Do you know why I stopped your vehicle?"

"Yes sir, I was speeding."

Check that box.

"Yes, you were. Do you know how fast you were speeding?"

"About seventy-five?"

Wow, this lady could have written her own ticket.

"Exactly! Is there any medical reason why you were speeding today?" I always asked that question just in case someone was headed to the hospital or in case they used that excuse later in traffic court.

"Yes...my turkey has hypothermia, officer!"

I wish I could have seen the look on my face, but it was certainly a WTF moment. "Excuse me?"

"My turkey has hypothermia!"

About that time, and you just cannot make this up, up from between her big breasted cleavage, popped a turkey head. Not just a little turkey mind you, this was a small Butterball sized bird climbing up and out of this lady's shirt! Then it started gobbling and jiggling her boobs!

"See! He is cold, and I have to get him to the vet because he has hypothermia!"

The bird was still gobbling away, jiggling boobs and working his way out of her shirt when I walked back to my car. I didn't know what to think, but I messaged my dispatchers over the computer and told them what was going on. Now I've met some interesting people on traffic stops, but a boob-jiggling turkey staying warm in this lady's shirt was off the charts. In fact, right then and there, I changed the title of this book.

And, oh...yes...I still wrote her a ticket, but only for nine over.

****

Every few years the forensic nurses from the Fairbanks Memorial Hospital will come to the police department and provide refresher training on administering sexual assault exam kits on suspects. These kits are designed to collect forensic evidence from sexual assault suspects in the field. For example, we collect head hair samples and pubic hair samples along with the not-so-pleasant penile swabs. The point of collecting the swabs is to try and collect the victim's DNA on the shaft of the suspect's penis. It is great evidence when a suspect denies having sexual intercourse with a victim and yet the victim's DNA is found in their penis.

The training is a little dry, no pun intended, so we try and make it as fun as possible. One time the nurses brought a big rubber dildo with a suction cup on the bottom to the training to physically show us how they like to swab penises in the emergency room.

One of the nurses took the dildo out of the box and plopped it down on the table.

Detective Nolan proclaimed, "Oh my God! That thing is *huge!*" And it really was. We were all thinking it, he just said it first.

A few minutes later, when I wasn't paying attention, Detective Elzey picked it up and when I looked up from my notebook, he smacked me across the face with it. We all shared a good laugh.

Later in the day, I got a call from a non-police officer buddy of mine.

"Hey man, how's your day? Anything cool going on?"

"Well, I got smacked in the face with a big rubber cock! How is yours?"

It is the only time in my life I have ever said that I was been smacked in the face by a big rubber dick.

****

Some of the training nurses provided came in useful on cases like what happened in February of 2008. An employee from a local fast food restaurant came forward and admitted that he and two other employees were planning on robbing and killing another employee. The plan was to hide and then ambush the employee when she opened the store the following morning. In her possession would be the morning money drop for the cash register. Our informant got cold feet and came to his senses the day before the robbery was to go down.

Technically these guys had not committed a crime—yet. Conspiracy cases are hard to prove, as often an actual crime has yet to be committed. Suspects need to take some type of overt action to further the commission of the crime they are conspiring to commit before we can arrest them. So we had a decision to make. We kicked around the idea of staking out the restaurant and swooping in like the A-Team when the suspects made their move. But what if we were too late, and they killed the clerk before we could get there?

The clerk, who we consulted with, was understandably not crazy about the idea.

We decided to wire up the informant. This involved taping a recording device on his body so we could record their conversations while they planned the robbery. Since all three were supposed to hang out that night anyway, the plan worked like a charm. I was paired up with one of my partners, Detective Chris Nolan, for the evening in a chase car. Our job was to follow the suspects in their car while they drove around town talking about the robbery. But we could not hear the live feed from the wire so we had no idea what they were discussing or where they were going. We had to rely on other detectives monitoring the wire to provide us this information.

At some point we were told to drive to the apartment complex where one of the suspects lived. The parking lot in front of the complex was full, so we pulled around back and found a parking spot behind the building. As we were sitting in the dark, radio chatter alarmed us that the suspect's vehicle was approaching the apartment complex. I looked around and mentioned to Chris that the only parking spot left was beside us. We looked either like cops or missionaries in our shirts and ties. We couldn't move, because by this time, we could see headlights bobbing up and down across the snow headed our way. I told him, "Listen, if that car pulls in beside us, I'm going to lean over and pretend I'm giving you a blow job. You just tip your head back and act like you are enjoying it."

"You're kidding right?"

"Hell no, you got a better idea?"

The headlights became brighter as they approached, and I whispered for Chris to get ready. About then I hear the *ziiiippppp* noise of his pants zipper headed south.

"What are you doing?" I demanded.

As the car passed in front of us Chris grabbed the back of my head and pulled me down into his crotch. I was screaming like a girl as he cracked up saying, "What the hell, it was your idea, so you'd better finish the job!"

Thankfully the suspects drove right on by.

As a side note, we ended up contacting the suspects later that evening and the two guys confessed to conspiring to rob and kill the clerk. The ring leader of the crew ended up having a really bad night. He started off the evening being arrested for conspiracy to commit murder, then when he was searched we found nearly an 8-ball of cocaine shoved down the side of his high-top tennis shoes.

As if that wasn't bad enough, the guy asked if we could run him by his house on the way to jail to pick up some medications he needed. I guess he forgot that his fourteen-year-old pregnant girlfriend was living with him.

****

Even though I was no longer a rookie, there was no shortage of job mishaps on my part. It was the winter of 2012 and I had been waiting a week to testify during a homicide trial. I had listened to the direct testimony of several of the State's witnesses and the relentless and sometimes monotonous questioning from the defense attorney. The trial was going in our favor and momentum seemed to be on our side, or so I believed. The jury seemed intrigued and engaged most of the time. Now it was my job to get up on the stand and tie the case together, to present the case like a carefully wrapped birthday gift with neat little bow on top to the jury. I was going to answer the questions that had been lingering for days and link the evidence collected at the scene to the suspect. Finally, I was going to explain every detail of the suspect's confession.

The first thing I did, and virtually the same thing I do every time I take the stand, was to pour myself a large cup of water. I become very dry-mouthed when I talk a lot, so instead of interrupting myself to pour water mid-sentence, I just get one ready to go as soon as I'm sworn in. All of my reports and notes I had taken to help with my testimony were laid out in front of me in a specific order. I was ready to go...it was game time.

The prosecutor began his inquiry asking about my background, training, experience as well as my current job duties. Just as he asked the first question about my investigation, I knocked over the full cup of water. Water ran all over my reports and off the table and into my lap. *Nice job Dumbass; well played.*

"Detective, did you understand the question?"

"Yes, sir, but uh, could I have moment to clean up the cup of water I spilled?"

The defense attorney looked amused. He was certainly enjoying watching the supposedly professional detective on the stand making a fool of himself. While I was soaking the water up from my lap and off the stand, it dawned on me maybe I could use the moment as an ice breaker between myself and the jury. I knew from jury selection that some of them had children, so I said, "Well, I guess I won't yell at my kids when they spill their drinks tonight at dinner!"

Most of the jurors laughed, and I even got a few smiles from the gallery. However, it wiped the smile off the defense attorney's face. I made it through one day of direct testimony before his client changed his plea to guilty mid-trial. Case closed and an embarrassing lesson learned.

****

I am convinced that being an effective interviewer takes time, patience, and lots of practice. An officer will never become a good interviewer if he doesn't jump right in the fire and spend a lot of time in the interview room with suspects. You learn by trial and error when to ask the hard questions, when to bluff and when not to, and when to start accusing the suspect of committing the crime. You must think on your feet and improvise quickly and be creative with the stories you tell suspects to make them feel more comfortable.

Improvising, rolling with the punches...it's all part of the job. One night on patrol we responded to a report of a burglary in progress at a multi-unit apartment complex. We caught a guy running from the building, but we didn't have any proof that he was running from the victim's apartment. We had dealt with this guy before, so I knew he wasn't exactly rowing his boat with both oars in the water. In other words, he was pretty dumb. He was sitting on the stairs inside the building being questioned by another officer when I walked in.

I interrupted them. "Carl, I know you were inside that apartment, so don't lie to me."

"I wasn't in there," he insisted.

"Fine, Carl, you wait right here, and I'm going to go back to the station and get my infrared footprint machine. Then, I'm going to come back here and scan the bottom of your foot. Then, I'm going to scan the carpet in the apartment you broke into, and it will tell me if your shoeprints are on the carpet."

He responded, "Well, what if I wasn't wearing shoes?"

I improvised. "Easy, I'll just attach the sock adapter to my infrared footprint machine and scan your sock and then scan the carpet. If your socks were on that carpet it will tell me so."

"Okay fine, I broke in there, but I wasn't alone."

Sometimes it is that easy.

One such interview comes to mind in which I may have gotten a little *too* creative. Patrol officers who have a vested interest in a case will often ask to sit in on the interview with the suspect. More often than not, I think this is a great idea because it tells me the officer wants to learn how to be a good interviewer and that he's trying to do his or her job better.

Officer Ace Adams[1] had taken a report from a male victim who said he had been sexually assaulted by another man that morning. The story went something like this - the suspect was a visiting professor from the Lower 48 doing a series of guest lectures at UAF. He and a group of students went out drinking one night after class. The group ended up crashing at the suspect's hotel room that night. The next morning, all of the students left except the victim who had passed out drunk in bed with the suspect the night before. One thing led to another, and the suspect ended up performing oral sex on the victim. The victim claimed he never told the suspect to stop touching him until the suspect tried to kiss him because he was scared to be kissed by another man.

My hunting partner and I had just finished giving a seminar on bear hunting at Sportsman's Warehouse when my lieutenant called me and told me to head into work to interview the suspect. I was pretty upset, because based on the circumstances, I thought the officer who took the report could handle the interview. But orders are orders, so I headed into work. I met with Ace, who told me the circumstances of the case.

I wasn't impressed. It seemed to me the victim didn't mind getting a blow job, but he balked when it came to kissing another man. Ace asked if he could sit in on the interview. I told him absolutely because I wanted to show him how to get a confession. He didn't think I could.

The suspect was huge, at least 6'4" and 350 pounds easy. He denied touching the other guy in any way sexually. We went back and forth for a little while, doing the yes-you-did, no-I-didn't routine.

Finally, I just stopped him cold and told him, "I know you did, and I know why. Let me guess, you're married right? Kids?"

He hung his head, "Yes."

---

1 Ace Adams is currently a detective with FPD.

"So, here you are, a long way from home, and you've always wanted to try being with another guy, always had that desire, but you've never had the chance because you're married."

He didn't say anything. He just stared at me. That's how I knew I was starting to press the right buttons.

"You woke up this morning, and this guy was in bed with you. You inch closer, he moves closer, hands start roaming, and before you know it, you're blowing the guy and there is nothing wrong with that."

He didn't say a word, and more importantly, he wasn't denying anything.

I continued, "I know that is what happened, because the same thing happened to me my freshman year of college with my roommate. I had always wanted to try being with another guy, but I never had the chance. Well, I guess we both felt that way because one night one thing led to another, and before you know it, I was blowing him."

I glanced over at Ace who had that deer in the headlights look on his face, and I prayed he stayed quiet.

"So, I know that is what happened here, but I need you to be honest with me. I don't think you raped anyone."

He finally broke his silence. "Yeah, that is what happened, but I didn't rape anyone. I thought he wanted it, too."

A few minutes later, we walked out of the interview room.

"I can't believe you told that guy the same thing happened to you back in college," Ace said. 'And he actually believed you!"

I couldn't resist saying, "Well, why do you automatically assume I was lying?"

He started to laugh, but stopped and got serious really quick. "You were...right?"

"What do you think?" I left it at that.

CHAPTER 2
TALES FROM THE NORTH POLE

Everyone has to start somewhere. With an academy certificate in one hand and a stack of student loans (25K worth) that equated to a college diploma in the other, I was ready to save the world. I spread resumés around and applied for police jobs all over Alaska, from Kotzebue to Ketchikan. By that time, I was working as a student Community Service Officer at the University Police Department on the UAF campus. I would be remiss if I did not take a moment to thank then Chief of Police Terry Vrabec for his unconditional support. Terry really helped me when I was trying to land my first job. At the time of this writing, Terry is the Deputy Commissioner for the Alaska Department of Public Safety. The law enforcement community is lucky to have him going to bat for all of us.[2]

In retrospect, I am so glad that I was not considered for some of the jobs I applied for. People are still using "honey buckets" as toilets in some of the communities I offered my services. If you aren't familiar with the intricacies of using honey buckets, you can research them on the internet, but make sure you click on the images tab. Just imagine a bucket being used as a repository in the absence of modern plumbing. Thankfully, they don't use honey buckets at the Santa Claus House, and that is exactly where my career began, at the North Pole Police Department on 125 Snowman Lane.

---

2 Since this writing, Terry Vrabec retired after serving the citizens of Alaska for more than twenty years.

Located approximately fourteen miles southeast of Fairbanks, the city of North Pole is on the small side with an official population of 2,220. Most locals refer to North Pole in a geographic sense, which covers the entire 99705 Zip Code. The "unincorporated city" of North Pole, ranging south from the Fairbanks city limits to Moose Creek on the Richardson Highway, would actually be one of the most populous cities in the state if it were incorporated. There are no counties in Alaska in the traditional sense, instead we have boroughs. Fairbanks and North Pole are both located in the Fairbanks North Star Borough (FNSB), and both cities provide law enforcement services within their city limits, while the Alaska State Troopers (AST) cover the unincorporated areas.

The city of North Pole is a summertime tourist destination that boasts the world's largest ceramic statue of Santa Claus. The Santa Claus House is a year round attraction for tourists and a favorite place for locals to take their children during the Christmas season. There are dozens of "Alaskana" history books out there on the region, so I'm not going to bore you with a discussion on the settling of the area. Growing up, kids from Fairbanks always thought folks who lived in North Pole were a little "off." And with the infamous reputation as the meth lab capital of the state, it's no wonder why. The running joke was they should put a fence around the city but leave the McDonalds on the outside so us "good and clean Fairbanks folk" can stop in on our way down the highway. All of this was no surprise to me when I started my job, as I'd grown up in Fairbanks.

I was sworn in on May 19th, 1999 as a patrol officer with the North Pole Police Department (NPPD). It wasn't much of a ceremony; there was no one there but me, the mayor, and the Chief of Police, Alan Ownby. I was the last officer Alan hired before he retired. As a parting gift he gave me a pair of well-used Smith and Wesson black hinge handcuffs with his initials engraved near the hinge. I guess he figured he didn't need them in retirement and they were better off in my belt than sitting in a box. I still keep the cuffs in my tactical vest, and they've seen a great deal more use since Alan gifted them to me.

It was a good thing he did, as the budget for the department back then had taken a hit, and good duty gear was hard to come by. My first ballistic vest had to be special ordered because the department only had a few *very* used vests in storage. The only spare they had sitting around that kind of fit was an old white expired piece of crap with no trauma plate. I had to safety pin and duct tape the straps across my chest every time I put that damn thing on. Not only was it not safe, it was humiliating and uncomfortable. But I made the best of it knowing my new vest was "on the way." Over six weeks later it finally arrived. I had quite the orgasmic experience pulling that vest over my head and sliding the straps across my chest, minus the safety pins and duct tape.

Even in a small town like North Pole, where officers are generally as busy as they want to be, the rookie-cop learning curve is fairly steep. Although the population and the city limits are very small, we were often requested to provide assistance for troopers working in unincorporated North Pole. Unlike some states, Alaska police officers have statewide jurisdiction, so our authority does not end at the city limit sign.

I remember those first couple weeks on the job clearly. Maybe because I was young, naïve, or just plain excited to finally be doing the job, but I was proud to be a police officer, and I was determined not to just be another badge and gun on the street. I was assigned a female field training officer, and my first call was to handle an abandoned snow machine out on the dyke behind the high school. Easy enough...call a tow truck, no report and clear. The first vehicle I pulled over was for speeding on 8th Avenue. The vehicle was a minivan, and the driver was a nice lady accompanied by her young daughter; I did not issue a citation. And I'm certain I was more nervous than she was.

My first arrest came at the end of my first week on the job. My Field Training Officer (FTO) and I received a tip that a guy by the name of J.R. was hiding out in his girlfriend's apartment. The apartment was located around the corner from the police station. I knocked on the door; he answered it and invited us into the apartment. I'm not sure if he just figured the game was up, or if he was even aware he was wanted. Regardless, he was taken into custody without much excitement. I would like to think it was my "command presence" that forced him to comply so easily, but in reality my hands were trembling when I slid the cuffs first on his right wrist, then his left. In retrospect there is no doubt he could tell I was a rookie, as this wasn't his first trip around the block. And this would not be the last time I would have the pleasure of arresting J.R., but I'll save that for later.

A couple weeks later, I was transferred to graveyard shift (midnight to 8 am), still riding with the same female FTO. The first evening was especially memorable. We were doing a bar check at a local watering hole named Blackie's Bar, a known Hells Angels hangout. My FTO recognized one of the guys in the bar as someone she thought had a warrant. Ironically, his last name was Lawless— no kidding. Dispatch confirmed the warrant was valid, and right then I knew I had a problem. I told my FTO I was going to escort the gentleman outside and hook him up. She was scared and didn't want to go inside the bar. I couldn't understand why. Isn't that what we were supposed to do? I was young and ready to brawl, so a bar full of bikers wasn't going to stop me. She reluctantly followed me inside the crowded bar.

Despite my FTO's misgivings, I walked up to the bar where Mr. Lawless sat nursing his Budweiser. He seemed to be having a rather personal connection with it, staring broodingly into the bottle opening, and I could tell that before I even reached him, his shoulders were tensed, his knuckles white. He didn't look at me, but I knew he knew I was there. When I rapped my knuckles on the bar counter and told him to meet me outside, I got that side-eye that told me I'd already said the wrong thing.

In retrospect, it could be perceived like I was calling him outside to fight and well, maybe that is what he thought too. Doubtless, he was sizing me up on the way to the door. I'm an average sized guy, six-foot and about 195 pounds. Suspects don't know if they can take you or not, so they have a decision to make and they make it quickly. If you act nervous at all or show any sign of weakness, their decision is easy; they think they can win. Suspects don't like fighting with female officers for obvious reasons, and they are usually smart enough not to scrap with officers sporting body builder physiques. Average-sized officers often end up as good candidates for fights.

As soon as we walked outside, I grabbed his arm, told him he was under arrest for a warrant, and the fight was on. He took a swing which I blocked, and then I threw him up against the front of his truck, which happened to be parked near the front door. He tried to elbow me a couple times, but I was able to get my hand wrapped around his head and take him to the ground hard. I put my shin across the guy's ear and put some weight on his head until he quit squirming around. And what was my FTO doing while this was going on? She was dancing around like she had to piss really bad while threatening the guy—and me—with pepper spray. She was in condition black; she had totally lost it. With Lawless flattened beneath me, I told her to calm down and to radio dispatch and request Alaska State Troopers (AST) to respond for help.

The nearest troopers were at the AST POST (headquarters) but they covered the 15 miles to North Pole in record time. I still remember the wonderful sound of that siren echoing on that cold winter night, becoming louder as they got closer as Lawless and I struggled on the ground. My FTO stood there yelling at Lawless to stop fighting but she never joined the fight. I was finally able to get on top of him and pin him to the ground. I was lucky that no one inside the bar knew what was happening outside. If some of his biker friends had come to his aid I would have been in real trouble.

The sound of the siren got closer and Trooper Pat Nelson, who was also in training with AST, slid to a stop in the icy parking lot and ran over to help. We got Lawless in cuffs and I was finally able to catch my breath. I needed to get into better shape. After fighting non-stop for what seemed like twenty minutes, I found myself gasping for air. I could have easily got my ass kicked if Lawless himself had been in better shape. It was a hard lesson learned but one I took to heart.

****

Shortly after the bar fight with Lawless, my first FTO was assigned to a different shift so I started riding with Mark. Though I was quickly learning the ropes, I still made the occasional rookie mistake. It's not uncommon to drive back and forth between North Pole and Fairbanks several times a shift. There is no jail or even a holding facility in North Pole, so whenever someone was arrested we drove into town to the Fairbanks Correctional Center (FCC). Sometimes the arrestee would post bail before we finished our booking paperwork. They would ask us for a ride back out to North Pole, only this time they would request to sit in the front seat.

Early one morning on graves, about a month into my training program, Mark and I made a DUI (driving under the influence) arrest - nothing out of the ordinary - just a run-of-the-mill DUI. After we finished processing the suspect at the station, Mark asked if I felt comfortable transporting the guy to Fairbanks. Having a bunch of paperwork to get caught up on, Mark figured I could stay out of trouble driving to Fairbanks and back. My strict instructions were: "Go straight there and back. No traffic stops, calls or anything, just straight there and back." No problem. Since the guy had been fully cooperative, I felt completely confident. Maybe a little overconfident.

We reached the Fairbanks Correctional Center(FCC) without incident, and I booked the guy in for his DUI. He was placed in a large holding cell, which was common until the correctional officers determined where he would be housed in one of the wings. In those days, we issued a driver's license revocation form to people arrested for DUI. We couldn't just give the form to them, we were required to read it aloud. I asked one of the correctional officers if he would unlock the door to the holding cell for me (which he did electronically) so I could pop my head in the cell and read this guy the revocation form.

I opened the door and reached back to catch the door as it closed behind me but missed. I felt like a total idiot because now I was locked in the holding cell with this guy. Through the window I saw the correctional officer chatting on the phone. I wasted no time knocking on the window of the cell. No response from the officer. I glanced at the guy I had just arrested, and I'd never seen such a large grin.

It was a Scooby Doo moment. "Rutt Roh Raggy!" I doubled my efforts banging on the window, and finally the officer noticed me. Still on the phone, he simply shook his head at me like a disappointed father—and he still hadn't unlocked the door! I think he was teaching the rookie a lesson. When the suspect stood up, still smiling from ear to ear, and started to walk toward me, the door lock finally popped.

That is the only time in my life I have ever been locked behind bars. And it was more than enough. I had learned my lesson and I never made it again.

****

I was still working for North Pole Police Department (NPPD) during the summer of 1999 when early one summer morning an AST unit pulled over an Air Force truck just outside the city limits of North Pole. I was still training with Mark, and since we didn't have anything going on, we headed that direction in case the trooper needed any assistance. When we arrived, the trooper told us he believed the driver was drunk. Since I was still in training he asked if we wanted to handle the DUI arrest. In all actuality this particular trooper was "retired on duty" with only about a month to go until he moved back into civilian life. He wasn't looking for any additional headaches his last month on patrol. Now that I've been in his shoes, I don't blame him one bit.

We agreed to take the arrest and the trooper left us with the driver still seated in the Air Force truck. As it turned out, the driver was a Navy SEAL temporarily assigned to Eielson Air Force Base for training along with the rest of his SEAL team. That evening, he decided to take an Air Force truck off base and get tanked. The trooper pulled him over before he had a chance to make it back on base, where he most likely would have been detained at the gate anyway. It was also his second DUI arrest, so in his mind I'm sure he was aware the choices he made that evening could ruin his career.

To be honest, this guy scared me. I had already fought with one drunk so I had an idea how volatile intoxicated people could be. But this guy was a Navy SEAL! Cautiously, I had him perform a series of field sobriety tests, which, while he didn't fail miserably, he still failed. With that in mind, I made the decision that I was going to arrest him, but before I did that I had to consult with Mark. I needed a few things ironed out before I jumped in on this one, after all, TASERs weren't standard issue yet.

I staged my consultation back at the cruiser while the SEAL leaned against the back of his truck, just out of earshot. "Mark, I'm going to arrest this guy."

In his easy-going way, he replied, "Well yeah, go ahead."

"What do you want to do if he fights? This guy would kill me." My hands were already shaking with adrenaline. I can handle myself, but this guy was way out of my league.

"Well, you go ahead, and I got your back."

"Fine." I offered my solution, "In that case, if he fights, I'm just going to shoot him. I mean, he's a trained killer, for Christ sake."

Mark gave the SEAL a cursory glance. "Good point."

Readying myself for a fight, I informed the man he was under arrest. And if he had gut-punched me, I couldn't have been more surprised at his reaction. In one of my first yet lasting impressions of humility, the man started crying when I put the cuffs on him. He begged me to let him go, pleading with me that I was ruining his career and that he would be kicked out of the SEALs because this was his second DUI arrest.

In that moment, I felt bad for the guy, I really did. I'm not a machine that is formatted to follow the letter of the law. I'm not programmed like that. In a career of firsts, this was a first. And for a moment, my resolve wavered. But then I asked myself: what if this guy had slammed his truck into another vehicle and killed someone? What if he killed someone I knew? What if by arresting him, we were preventing him from driving drunk in the future? I realize those are a lot of what ifs, but in reality, officers are forced to make decisions like this routinely. Did I personally alter the course of this man's life? I suppose, but in reality he did it to himself.

****

Because of the low call volume on graves in North Pole, we spent most of our time pursuing DUI Violators. One night I pulled up to a gas pump next to a guy filling his "crotch rocket" racing motorcycle. The only problem was he was filling it with diesel. I asked the guy, "Uh...sir...you do know you're filling that up with diesel, right?" The look on his face was priceless, like someone had kicked him in the gut. He was obviously trashed. I don't know what ended up costing more: the fines and jail time associated with the DUI arrest or fixing his brand new motorcycle.

****

On a beautiful July morning in 1999, North Pole dispatch received several 9-1-1 calls about a car driving *southbound* in the *northbound* lane toward North Pole. Luckily it was a Sunday morning so there wasn't much traffic on the highway. Fourteen miles of driving on the wrong side of the highway is impressive. I managed to get the car pulled over as it came *off* the *entrance* ramp into North Pole. The driver, I will call him by his initials C.D. was absolutely, falling-down-drunk hammered.

After he completed some semblance of field sobriety tests, including pissing all over himself, Mark and arrested him for DUI and drove him back to the station so he could blow in to the Intoximeter (the instrument being used at the time). During the process, he wanted to make a phone call, which we were required to allow him to do. He called his uncle and told him he had been arrested. His uncle asked where he had been arrested. "I'm in the North Pole with Santa Claus and his little elf...ho ho ho."

In case you're wondering, Mark was Santa Claus.

****

North Pole Police Department was a great place to begin my career, but there was no way I was spending twenty-plus years driving in circles around the Santa Claus House. For most officers, NPPD is a great place to start or finish a career. You can be as busy as you want to be and gain some invaluable experience or just coast on through a couple years doing very little pro-active police work until retirement.

I had been working in North Pole less than a year when I received a call from Fairbanks Police Chief, James "Scooter" Welch. Scooter told me that FPD had an opening and he was wondering if I was interested in applying. Of course, I jumped at the opportunity, and within a couple months, I was offered a patrol officer position with FPD.

I never thought I would live in Fairbanks after high school, much less begin a career that would keep me here for the foreseeable future. But it's funny how things work out. That high school sweetheart that kept me in Alaska after graduation has no idea how she changed my life and set me on a course for what has become a roller coaster of a career. I only wish she hadn't scribbled so much in my senior yearbook.

CHAPTER 3
THE EARLY YEARS

Transitioning from North Pole to Fairbanks was smooth, mostly because I already knew most of the officers and I had a year on the streets under my belt. Orientation with the city wasn't a problem because I grew up in Fairbanks. Learning the hundred blocks and the side streets in industrial South Fairbanks was a chore, but I managed. I was proud to put on that dark blue uniform. I still remember standing in the dark locker room at the old station on 6th Avenue, staring at myself in a mirror and being proud of what I had accomplished. FPD was a busy department, and I was ready for whatever the Golden Heart City had to throw at me.

In those days, working at FPD was an honor, and it was extremely hard to get hired. When I tested right out of the academy, there were so many people taking the written exam that the department had to use a lecture hall on the University of Alaska Fairbanks campus to hold everyone. FPD was, and still is, a very well-respected department. I suppose this is true for law enforcement agencies across the country; the glory days of lecture halls filled with applicants are over.

****

Officer Chris Nolan ended up in training with me, and we handled a lot of calls together. Chris and I would end up spending nearly thirteen years in investigations together working violent crimes[3]. The second call I responded to with FPD while on swing shift was a subject removal call from a shady apartment complex in midtown Fairbanks. Chris, who was training on the same shift with a different FTO, also responded. Normally, rookies in training would not handle calls so early in training, but a lot was expected of me because of my prior experience.

The caller answered the door. Butt naked, he reeked of beer and slurred every word he spoke. When he turned around, there was a stream of feces from his buttocks down his leg. As we asked a few questions, it became apparent what he wanted and what had happened. He was mad because the guy inside had "pulled out" too soon causing the mess. So yeah, he wanted him out of his apartment.

Welcome to Fairbanks and the Fairbanks Police Department. It was nothing like North Pole!

****

In July of 2002, I was working swing shift patrol on the south side of Fairbanks. I had a ride-along that night, a young girl who was a student at West Valley High School in Fairbanks. She was working on a project for school, and two of the requirements were to interview a police officer and observe their duties and activities for one shift. Lucky for her, it had been a busy and interesting night. Another officer and I had scuffled with a guy at Denny's at the beginning of the shift, and we had been going call-to-call since.

I was driving north on Cushman Street, toward downtown, when I saw a guy I recognized get out of a car in the Thrifty Liquor parking lot. The guy was J.R., the first person I had ever arrested as a cop in North Pole. I radioed dispatch to run him for any warrants. Sure enough, there was an outstanding misdemeanor warrant for his arrest. I pulled in the parking lot and told my ride-along to stay in the car.

Then I screwed up. I approached J.R. and asked if I could speak with him outside. He said sure, and we walked out the entrance together.

I told him, "You have a warrant for your arrest."

I don't think the "est" at the end of "arrest" left my lips before he took off like a gazelle running across the savannah. I should have

---

3 Chris Nolan retired from FPD in 2015 after 20 years of service. He also spent 24 years serving in both the United States Army and Alaska Air Guard. We are still close friends and live near each other in Idaho.

just arrested him inside the liquor store. Not wanting to look like a complete fool, I took off running after him, yelling back at my rider, "Stay in the car and lock the doors!"

Now, I don't run. I kick ass on an elliptical machine, but I don't actually run anywhere. When I was born, and as you recall I was born in the South, the doctor who delivered me told my parents, "Man, those are the flattest feet on any white kid I have ever seen!" So, I don't run, but I was going to at least look like I was trying.

I chased him south on Cushman Street before he took a right turn on 16th Avenue. I was losing ground quickly, and in the back of my mind, I knew there was no way in hell I was ever going to catch him. That's when a car pulled up beside me. At first, I thought it was J.R.'s buddy going to pick him up, but it wasn't. I looked over and the driver had slowed down and pushed open the passenger door.

"Hey, get in, dude!" he yelled.

I kept running.

The car crept along beside me because, well, I wasn't running very fast.

"Seriously man, get in. Let's get him!"

Abandoning my misgivings, I jumped in the passenger seat and my new "partner" hit the gas and sped up to J.R. I jumped from the still moving car like a stunt man in an action movie and tackled him like a football player. He was worn out, and I had savored the chance to catch my breath. I cuffed him and looked back at the driver who was giving me a big thumbs up! Then he shut the passenger door and drove off. I have no idea who he was.

J.R. managed to spit out, "Damn, how did you catch me?"

As smartass as I could make it sound, I said, "Never run from the PO-lice!"

****

During my third week of training, my Fairbanks FTO, John Terland[4], and I got into a kick-ass pursuit. A young man was driving around the city shooting at passing cars, and 9-1-1 calls flooded in reporting him. One of FPD's units located his vehicle and tried to get him to pull over. Of course, he took off, and the pursuit was on. We

---

4 Jon Terland left FPD in 2003 and moved to Oregon where he served as a deputy sheriff and an Oregon Bureau of Land Management (BLM) Ranger. He is currently an academy instructor with the Department of Homeland Security.

chased him all over town before he headed south on the Richardson Highway toward North Pole. With me behind the wheel, John and I caught up to the pursuit. After a few U turns and changes in direction, we ended up being the second vehicle behind the suspect's car.

He pulled down Faultline Avenue on the way to North Pole. Our dispatcher advised that the road dead ended, so I was already thinking we were either going to shoot it out with this guy or he was going to take off running. Honestly, I was excited as hell. I was twenty-two years old and running balls-to-the-wall after some psycho with a gun who had been shooting at people. Words cannot describe the adrenaline rush.

Finally, the suspect reached the end of the road. The patrol car in front of John and me rammed the driver's door of the suspect's vehicle just as I put our vehicle in park. As I was opening my door, I heard John fire at least two shots. Simultaneously, I looked to my left and my mouth nearly fell open. One of our investigators stood, his tactical shotgun leveled at the suspect's car, all while wearing a white t-shirt and plaid pajamas. All I could think was, "What in the hell?" But I didn't have time to ask.

The other pursuing officer, John, and I ran up to the car and pulled the suspect from the front seat and handcuffed him. When we put it all together later, John had seen the suspect raise his gun, and thinking he was going to take a shot at the other officer who had rammed his door, John fired off two shots. We gave him a lot of crap over the years for this, but he missed the whole damn car both times!

It turned out that the suspect was raising the gun to shoot himself in the head, but he chickened out and ducked when he pulled the trigger. There was a gash on his head, he was higher than a kite, but he would be fine.

The pursuit had ended in our investigator's front yard. As he later described, "I was sitting there watching porn, and dispatch called and yelled that a pursuit was going to end in my front yard! I told my dog to get down, and I grabbed my shotgun."

And in case that wasn't enough, it ended up that the suspect was a guy I'd attended high school with.

You just cannot make this stuff up.

****

During the summer of 2003, I was working DUI enforcement overtime, and I pulled over a car on the Old Steese Highway for nothing more than a headlight out. The vehicle quickly pulled into the parking lot of a bar in the area and the suspect took off on foot. As I said before, I am not a runner, but I couldn't say no to the chase.

I took off after the guy, following him into the bar, straight through and right out the back door. Then he ran back around to the front of the bar and right back out the back door. It was like a damn cartoon as back into the bar we went. Only this time, the runner, who was not little, turned around and the fight was on. While we were rolling around on the ground in the bar, all I could hear was the bartender yelling at everyone else in the bar, "Don't help the cop! Don't help him!" To this day, it still makes me angry.

To make it worse, the suspect wriggled away from me, once again ran out the back and around the front of the bar to jump into his vehicle. The pursuit was on after that, but it was short-lived. He crashed his car just up the road on the Steese Highway near Farmers Loop.

I was thrilled to arrests this guy and charge him with everything from felony DUI to three counts of Drunk on a Licensed Premises. I mean really, technically every time he ran into the bar, he was committing another crime because he was drunk. After that, the rest of the shift went and arrested the bartender.

And for the next month, night shift did bar checks there every night and made several arrests. Karma.

****

I remember the call that confirmed my belief that I wanted to be a detective and that showed me I had real potential at being an effective interviewer. Investigator Matt Soden[5] and I were called to an apartment complex in midtown after a concerned neighbor saw two guys carrying an intoxicated female into an apartment.

The neighbor did not recognize the female and thought it was suspicious, and they were worried about her safety. When we arrived on scene, we listened at the door to hear a female moaning inside. We banged on the door, and of course, no one answered, but we could hear someone scampering around. I was about to boot

---

5 Matt Soden retired as the Acting Deputy Chief at FPD after 25 years of service. He is now the co-owner of a construction company in Fairbanks. On his last day at FPD, his final act was pinning on my LT. bars.

the door down when one of the guys finally opened it. There were condom wrappers on the floor, and this poor girl was passed out on the couch. The men had done a poor job of dressing her before answering the door. The worst thing was her age: she was thirteen.

Matt and I interviewed these two guys for hours. It seems simple right? The victim is thirteen years old, so just lock them up like on TV. But in the real world, you have to prove a crime took place. In this case, we had to prove that they had sex with her and that they knew or at least had a reasonable belief how old she was.

It took a while, but both guys ended up admitting they thought the girl was under sixteen (the age of consent at the time) and that they both had sex with her.

The interview was exhausting, but the satisfaction of knowing that the outcome was the tipping point that will put away two sexual predators was plain awesome.

And in a strange twist of fate, after they were released from prison, one of these guys killed himself on a motorcycle driving too fast around a curve. Karma had struck again.

CHAPTER 4
BLOOD MONEY

During the summer of 1901, the sternwheeler *S.S. Lavelle Young* made its way upstream through the narrow banks of the Chena River. The boat ran aground in shallow water about seven miles from the confluence of the Chena and Tanana Rivers. A man named Captain E.T. Barnette and his party disembarked with their supplies. Barnette's intention had been to travel upstream along the Chena River to Tanana Cross, where the Valdez-Eagle Trail crossed the Tanana River. Smoke rising from the boat's engines caught the eye of two miners in the nearby hills to the north. Their names were Felice Pedroni (an Italian immigrant better known as Felix Pedro) and his mining partner, Tom Gilmore.

Pedro and Gilmore followed the smoke to the banks of the Chena River and met Barnette and his men. Pedro believed there was gold in the hills to the north, and the two men convinced Barnette to establish a trading post for prospectors. If the large gold deposits he believed existed were unearthed, the Tanana Valley would be flooded with prospectors establishing mines and gold dredging operations. It was a long journey to Alaska's interior, and all those miners dreaming about gold nuggets and getting rich would need to be re-supplied once they reached the Tanana Valley. And he was right. On July 22, 1902, Felix Pedro struck gold in a creek about twelve miles north of Barnette's trading post on the Chena River. The city of Fairbanks was named after a senator from Indiana and soon to be Vice President during Theodore Roosevelt's second term (1905-1909), Charles W. Fairbanks, and was incorporated in 1903.

The first Fairbanks Police officer to lose his life in the line of duty was Chief of Police Alvin G. Miller. He was shot and killed on November 2, 1908 while responding to a report of a barricaded subject inside a hotel. Chief Miller was shot as he entered the room after breaking down the door.

In 1951 a pioneering Fairbanks resident named Kay Kennedy started the Golden Days Festival. Golden Days has since become an annual event that lasts five days and celebrates the history of Fairbanks and the gold rush that put Fairbanks on the map. There are races, parades, car shows, a Rubber Ducky Race down the Chena River, a lumber jack competition, and a variety of other events and activities that encapsulate the rich history of the city. But by far, the largest and most attended event is the Golden Days Parade.

Stretching out for more than two miles, the parade includes over one hundred floats, bands, dancers and all sorts of attractions. The parade is the grand finale of Golden Days. Some years the parade has started on Fort Wainwright and ended on the other side of town at Pioneer Park. Other years the parade began in the large parking lot behind the Carlson Center, our large sports arena, and went the opposite direction.

I've always enjoyed the parade, and when I was promoted in 2005, it came with the benefit of weekends off. I looked forward to finally watching the parade from the sidelines with my family in 2006 instead of working traffic control.

On July 22, 2006, the sun, which barely dips below the horizon during the short Alaskan summer, rose for another beautiful Saturday in the Golden Heart City. The Golden Days parade was scheduled to begin at about 10:00 A.M., and by 6:00 A.M., a few people, mostly event workers, had started to assemble behind the Carlson Center. An employee of the Fairbanks Chamber of Commerce was walking along the bike path between the Carlson Center and Pioneer Park[6]. The path winds along the banks of the Chena River, where she made a grisly discovery.

The 9-1-1 call came in around 6:15 A.M. My phone rang at about 6:30 A.M. When I saw the name "Dusty" on my caller ID, I

---

6 Formerly called "ALASKA LAND" Pioneer Park is a 44-acre Alaska heritage, cultural and theme park located in Fairbanks. It opened in 1967 to celebrate the centennial anniversary of the purchase of Alaska from Russia. Some of the park's main attractions are the Tanana Valley Railroad Museum, the *S.S. Nenana* sternwheeler, the Pioneer Museum and the Alaska Native Village.

knew right away I'd be heading to work. Lt. Don "Dusty" Johnson was my unit supervisor[7].

"Peyton, this is Dusty."

"Yeah, Dusty, what's up?"

"Patrol is dealing with a body by the river next to the Carlson Center. Can you go check it out?"

Since I was on call that weekend, I knew I didn't have a choice in the matter. "Sure thing, I'll call you when I find something out."

The 9-1-1 call was logged at 6:12 A.M. The written statement she provided reads as follows:

> "I was walking over to Pioneer Park from the Carlson Center back parking lot (along the river walk). I saw a man lying on the ground, thinking he was passed out. As I got closer, I saw a pool of blood on the ground and then on his head and on his arm. I called 911 then."

According to the report, the day shift watch commander and two patrol officers had responded to the scene and located the body along the bike path in some tall grass between the Carlson Center and the river. Fairbanks Fire Department paramedics also responded to the scene. While the officers were roping off the area to secure the scene, the paramedics rolled the man onto his back and attached heart monitor leads to his chest only to find no cardiac activity.

From the way Dusty had made it sound, the body was most likely a homeless person down by the river, not an uncommon occurrence even in the summer. Alcohol and exposure are the common denominators in most transient deaths in Fairbanks. I just assumed I was going to the scene to make sure no foul play was suspected in the death and that I would be home in time to go to the parade with my wife, Kristi and our two boys.

When I arrived at the Carlson Center, I took one look at the scene and knew this wasn't just an intoxicated homeless guy that drank himself to death by the river. The body was that of a young Alaska Native male whose face was covered in blood. From the direction the blood was flowing, I could tell he had originally been lying face down. Blood had pooled in the grass prior to the body being rolled and had run down to the bike path forming another

---

7 Lt. Don "Dusty" Johnson retired from FPD in 2007 after serving for nearly 30 years.

pool at its edge. He was wearing a white T-shirt and blue jeans. On his right foot was a blue Nike flip-flop. The left flip-flop was lying in the middle of the bike path some distance away from the body. There were clumps of green grass gripped tightly in his hands, like he'd been crawling through the grass before he died. I called Dusty and told him we were looking at a homicide and requested the rest of the team respond. Then I called my wife and told her the bad news.

While waiting on the rest of our team to arrive, I photographed and videoed the scene. More photos would be taken later once items of evidence were marked and collected. Dusty, Detective Dave Elzey and Investigator Peal Holston arrived on scene within the hour. It's very easy to get tunnel vision at a homicide scene and focus too closely on the area immediately around the body. All too often, we review death cases where officers take fifty pictures of the body but maybe five of the rest of the scene. Keeping that in mind, we began our search for clues on the bike path near the left flip-flop. Whatever event caused our victim to lose his shoe happened there.

We found blood in the grass near the left flip-flop. The drop was the first in a trail of blood leading to the body through the grass. There were impressions in the grass where you could tell he had crawled away from his attacker. Although his face was covered in blood, there were no obvious signs of a cause of death. Usually when someone is shot in the head, you can tell very easily they died from a gunshot wound to the head because half their head is gone or there are at least entry and or exit holes. If they are stabbed there are knife wounds, etc.

A closer scrutiny showed us that his left eye socket was deformed a bit and didn't look quite right. I noticed a small hole in his left ear just above the lobe. It almost looked like someone had ripped an earring out.

Other than a couple of cigarette butts on the bike path, we did not find much other evidence at the scene. In some bushes nearby, we found a red bicycle that we seized, but had no idea if it had anything to do with the homicide yet. After consulting with the State of Alaska Medical Examiner's Office, we rolled the body to examine his back for any signs of trauma. There was nothing obvious. Searching his pockets, we found his wallet in one and a cell phone in the other. His social security card, as well as other documents, identified him as Gary Lee Wilson Titus. He was from Minto, Alaska, a small, predominately Alaska Native community located on the Elliot Highway about a 120 mile road trip from Fairbanks. He was twenty-two years old.

Using long cotton swabs, I crawled through the grass collecting individual blood samples. The cotton swabs were packaged individually in case the blood came from someone other than the victim.

We took scale measurements of the scene using a long tape measure stretched down the bike path as a base line. The measurements ensured we could re-create the scene at a later time if needed for court. After several hours of measuring, photographing and collecting evidence, the request was made for the on-call funeral home to respond to the scene. Gary's body was taken from the scene to the Fairbanks Memorial Hospital where technicians had agreed to X-ray the body and look for foreign objects or clues as to what might have killed him. I was informed I would receive the results via email in a couple of hours.

We left an officer at the scene and went to the station to figure out what we were going to do next. After the early morning call and the long morning, I really needed some coffee. There were no witnesses to the murder, at least none that had come forward yet. We had to contact Gary's next of kin. Our dispatchers began running Gary's name through our computer systems searching for the names of people Gary may have been associated with when contacted by law enforcement. About that time I received an email from Fairbanks Memorial Hospital (FMH). Attached to the email were several X-rays. What I saw freaked me out.

"Guys, come look at this!" I shouted.

The group strolled over to my desk and huddled around my computer. They didn't say anything.

"Check it out!" I insisted.

Finally, Dave said, "What are you looking at? I only see a skull."

I wasn't sure how to respond. "Dave, look, there is a damn zipper in his face! Look! A freaking zipper right in the middle of his head! How in the hell did that get there? No wonder he's dead."

They all just looked at me like I was flipping crazy. Slowly, it dawned on me. The body was still inside the bag when they ran it through the X-ray machine.

I really needed some coffee. After a good laugh we took a closer look at the X-rays of Gary's head. There were pieces of shrapnel scattered throughout his skull cavity. He had been shot in the head, my guess was with a .22 caliber round. I couldn't tell how many times, but it was certain that hole in his ear lobe was a bullet hole. The bullet must have traveled through the lobe directly into his ear canal. We didn't see any shell casings at the scene, but then again we did not search the high grass very well.

As luck would have it, we did not have to wait long to get our first break in the case. I was studying the X-ray photos and downing my third cup of coffee when the phone rang.

"Good morning, Detective Merideth," I answered.

"Peyton, hey this is Stanley[8]. The word on the street is my cousin Gary got shot last night." Stanley and I had attended UAF together, and we had stayed in touch after graduation. Like Gary, he was an Alaska Native from Minto. Gary's next of kin had not been notified yet, but I had to gamble a bit here and show my hand. We hadn't released any details to anyone about the homicide, so Stanley most likely had some good information.

"Yeah, Stanley, sure looks that way. But listen, I haven't been able to contact Gary's parents yet, so keep this quiet. I'm sorry about your cousin, but I need some help figuring out what happened."

Stanley told me he would contact the village elders in Minto and arrange for them to inform Gary's mother in-person about his death with instructions to call my cell phone when she felt up to it. He also told me that several of his cousins had been with Gary when he was shot, but they had not told anyone but him about what had happened.

The kids weren't scared of retribution from the shooter, and it wasn't that they didn't like the police. Instead of calling 9-1-1 or running for help, they chose to wait for the police to find them. Common sense would dictate that out of six shooting witnesses, one of them would have gone for help. Instead, they just ran home and went to bed. But this is not an uncommon occurrence among young

---

8 Stanley is a fictitious name. He is now deceased. We really did attend college together and his actions in this case are based on fact.

Alaska Native men, and I'm not sure why. It's a cultural thing and one I have come to accept over the course of my career.

For example, a couple years after this incident, I was called out to investigative a double homicide that occurred in a wooded area in South Fairbanks. Five or six young Alaska Native youths had gone to the movies together and were hanging out in the woods, probably smoking, when one kid took a stolen pistol out of his pocket. As it turned out, two of the kids had been dating and had recently broken up. The young lady was dating another guy who was hanging out in the group that night. The scorned ex-boyfriend asked to see the gun. He tried to load it but couldn't figure out how to work the action, so he asked another kid to load it for him. The other kid loaded the gun and handed it back. The ex-boyfriend said, "Thanks," raised the gun, and shot his ex-girlfriend and her new man in the head at point blank range. He chased after the other kids who ran off into the night. When he couldn't catch them, he shot himself in the middle of the street. None of the other kids told anyone, called 9-1-1 or told their parents when they got home. Their parents had to wake them up when we came knocking. I just don't get it. But, after many cases like these, I have learned to think twice about pre-judging people who don't call 911. They don't always have ulterior motives for not calling the police.

Returning to Gary's case, it was about fifteen minutes after Stanley called that Detective Elzey[9] and I met him at a residence in the Birch Park apartment complex on Stewart Street. There we contacted A.A. and L.N., potential witnesses to Gary's murder. Stanley made the introductions and assured the young men that we could be trusted. I spoke with A.A. in private while Detective Elzey interviewed L.N.

Both men were in town for the World Eskimo Indian Olympics, better known around here as WEIO, which were being held at the Carlson Center during this time. First held during Golden Days week in 1961, WEIO is both a celebration and competition where athletes compete in traditional Eskimo and American Indian games and tests of endurance and skill. Residents of small communities around the state travel to Fairbanks to enjoy the games and the marketplace where Alaska Natives sell their handmade traditional crafts. My

---

9 Dave Elzey retired from FPD in 2018 after 20 years of service. We spent 10 years together in investigations.

personal favorite is the seal skinning competition. They actually haul out dead seals and skin them on the floor at what is normally center ice at the Carlson Center. One night they are playing NCAA hockey on the rink, and the next night they are skinning seals. Only in Fairbanks.

Early that morning, A.A. and a group of friends and cousins were walking around town when Gary called a guy named "Little Dave." He arranged to meet him behind the Carlson Center to buy some marijuana. Sometime between 5:00 and 6:00 A.M., they met Little Dave, who rode up on a bicycle. A.A. described Little Dave as "offended" at the presence of the group and felt they were going to jump him. At the time, I didn't understand what he meant or why Little Dave thought he was going to be jumped. It made more sense later when I learned that Gary did not have any money to pay for the drugs. I guess what A.A. was trying to say was that Little Dave felt disrespected.

A.A. and rest of the group hung back a bit while Gary met with Little Dave along the bike path. At some point Little Dave walked back to his bicycle but stopped and pulled out a handgun. The gun was black with neon-colored sights. He shot Gary in the head, but Gary didn't die right away. The rest of the group took off running, but A.A. saw Little Dave continue shooting at Gary. Little Dave was a white guy, short, maybe 5'5" to 5'8" wearing a red shirt and bluish-gray cutoffs or shorts. He had large tattoo on his arm that read "Blood Money" which he proudly showed off.

The story that L.N. told to Detective Elzey was virtually the same. L.N. added that their group had first met Little Dave near the footbridge across from Lathrop High School a few hours before the shooting. Over the next couple hours, Detective Elzey and I tracked down and interviewed all of the guys who were with Gary when he was shot. All of them told the same story with little variations here and there. The subtle differences let us know they had not put their heads together and fabricated a story.

We went back to the scene armed with a metal detector to look for shell casings. We initially found five, but a couple days later a sixth was discovered. The .22 caliber casings were scattered around the scene tucked beneath the tall grass. They would have been impossible to find without the metal detector. If you were not looking for them, like when we initially worked the scene, you would have never found them. The first five casings were discovered on the Carlson Center side of the bike path away from the river. I was puzzled because there should have been one near the flip-flop down the path from where Gary died. That was where the first shot was fired, when Gary turned and was shot in the side of the head and came out of his flip-flop. The missing sixth casing was found a couple of days later on the river side of the path right where it should have been. I just missed it the first time.

By midday, we had explored most of the avenues at our disposal attempting to identify Little Dave, and we were quickly running out of options. We ran the moniker through all the data bases we could think of, and then ran the "Blood Money" tattoo with the same results: nothing. I was beginning to think our suspect was not from Alaska. I even called the Department of Corrections (DOC) to see if they had a record for a former inmate with a tattoo that read "Blood Money" on his right forearm. Nothing. I was hoping DOC would give us something, because most people are arrested a time or two before they jump right into the big leagues and kill someone. If this guy had a criminal record, it wasn't in Alaska. If he was a juvenile, that would make him even harder to identify because most juvenile records are sealed, even from law enforcement, without cutting some serious red tape. My only hope was that because he had a tattoo he was at least eighteen years old. In Alaska anyone being tattooed has to be at least 18.

I called home and spoke to Kristi for a few minutes. She and the boys had a great time at the parade although she was really sorry I was not able to make it—again. Kristi understood that I had an important job to do, and that sometimes the job got in the way of family activities. I filled her in on our progress, and she offered some words of encouragement that we would find our guy one way or another. At least we had a description of the suspect and the tattoo was a dead giveaway. Although I was frustrated that we didn't have a name, I was very optimistic our guy would turn up sooner rather than later.

Back at the station, I pulled Gary's cell phone out of the evidence bag that had been sitting on my desk since we returned from the scene that morning. We knew that Gary had exchanged calls with Dave prior to the homicide, so perhaps Dave's voice or his phone number was still stored in Gary's phone. I wondered how many times Gary's mother had tried calling him. Cell phone forensics was in its infancy in 2006, so I examined Gary's phone the old fashioned way: I turned it on, being extra careful not to erase anything. The voicemail box was full, but there were two new messages that hadn't been heard. The first message was left by a female and it clearly had nothing to do with the case. There was a second voicemail message received by Gary's phone at 5:51 A.M. The number that called was from a 407 area code. Florida.

"Hey, this Little Dave man where you at? I'm at the Carlson Center man where you at? Hit me back, you know my number, 407... peace."

Florida. Well now it made sense why we couldn't identify the guy in any Alaska databases. Because it was still the weekend, I knew we couldn't get any phone records for a Florida cell phone until Monday at the earliest. Hopefully, the suspect's name would be attached to the account information. But I didn't want to wait until Monday to find out who our guy was. Forty-eight hours is a long time. He could be anywhere in the country by Monday if he had the means and desire to leave the state. We kicked around the idea of calling the number, an idea that had pros and cons. I bet we tossed around making the call for an hour before I finally said, "What the hell, why not?" I hooked a recorder up to my desk line and made the call, which promptly went straight to an automated voicemail. Well, that was anticlimactic.

We had been beating the street all day in a desperate attempt to uncover the identity of the shooter, and I was dragging by 7:00 P.M. Dusty and I drove back to the Carlson Center. The evening festivities and games for WEIO were just getting under way. Over 2000 people had poured into the Carlson Center looking forward to a fun night of competition. I asked the event coordinator if he would mind if I made an announcement. I explained to him the circumstances, and he had no issues and granted my request. By this time, we were out of ideas and this was the last trick I had up my sleeve. I walked up the stairs on to the stage and stood in front of the microphone.

The last time I stood in front of a crowd this big at the Carlson Center was prior to the 1994 state championship high school basketball game. I was a junior in high school, and I had been asked to sing the National Anthem before the game, which was really cool because it was Trajan Langdon's last high school game. He played for East Anchorage High School, but he was headed to Duke University that fall to play for Coach K and the Blue Devils. His nickname at Duke was the Alaskan Assassin. After a successful college career, he spent twelve years in the NBA and in Europe. So there I was, a dozen years later taking the microphone once again under extremely different circumstances, unable to help but think of him. It's weird how things work out.

I cleared my throat and spoke slowly. My voice echoed through the building as I spoke. "Ladies and gentlemen, my name is Peyton Merideth, and I am a detective with the Fairbanks Police Department." People were still chattering in the stands. Not everyone was paying attention. I continued, "As many of you may have heard by now, a young man from Minto was murdered early this morning right outside of the Carlson Center." Crickets. That got their attention. "We have worked hard to develop a person of interest in this case, but we need your help finding him. He is a short, young white male with a large tattoo that says 'Blood Money' on his right forearm. If any of you know this person please call 9-1-1 or come to the stage and I will speak with you in private. Thank you for your help."

It would have been amazing to look out across the sea of people and see our guy jump out of his seat and head for an exit. Unfortunately that did not happen. That would have been too easy. I walked off stage and chatted with the event security for a few minutes while I waited for anyone who may know something to approach us. A couple of young men spoke with Dusty who said they knew who Little Dave was and that he hung out at an apartment off Clarkson in the University West neighborhood. They did not know his real name, but they did say he had a tattoo on his arm that said "Blood Money." We left after a bit and decided to call it a night. I was stressed out and exhausted, and I was looking forward to getting home and spending some time with my family before I passed out, only to do it again tomorrow.

It was about 9:00 P.M. when I walked through the door. I was greeted with big hugs from my two boys. They were in their pajamas. I made it home just in time to see them before bed. They were only four and three years old at the time. In their own language, the one only people with young kids can understand, they told me all about the parade and how much fun they had. And then the phone rang.

"Peyton, hey, this is Dan." That would be Chief of Police, Dan Hoffman[10]. Dan was a well-respected administrator and virtually everyone enjoyed working for him. During homicide investigations, he liked to be kept in the loop but never questioned our investigative approach or pestered us with questions when he knew we were busy.

"Hey, Chief, what can I do for you?" I replied.

"My daughter thinks she knows the guy you are looking for. He has a tattoo on right arm right? 'Blood Money' or something? She works with him at Chili's. His name is David Cox. I was in the stands at the Carlson Center when you made the announcement."

"You're kidding me?" I wasn't sure what else to say. What were the odds the guy we had been searching for high and low all day worked with the chief's daughter? I guess pretty good! "Thanks, Chief, I'll get on it." Kristi could tell I was excited when I hung up the phone. I kissed her goodbye and just like that, I was leaving again. I knew it was going to be a long night.

I updated Dusty, who agreed to meet me back at the office. It was 11:30 P.M. The night manager at Chili's was still working when I called. He confirmed the day shift manager had fired Cox that afternoon after he had been caught stealing and drinking alcohol from behind the bar. To ensure Cox had not concealed any bottles in his backpack, the manager searched it before Cox left and found a handgun. Of course, the manager had no idea that just a few hours before he was fired, Cox had committed a murder. He let him go with the handgun. If the manager had just called the police and reported the alcohol theft, the case would have been wrapped up in hours. Judging someone's actions in hindsight is easy, but to second-guess them is counterproductive during a homicide investigation when the clock is ticking. We pushed forward.

We got lucky again. We learned from the manager of Chili's that Cox had moved to Fairbanks from Florida to live with his mother and stepfather at the beginning of the summer. We ran his name through the Alaska Public Safety Information Network (APSIN) and got a hit. Cox was just eighteen years old, and it showed an address, most likely his mother's, on Antoinette Avenue on the north side of Fairbanks. We were rolling now, and I started to get excited. I felt the

---

10 Chief Dan Hoffman retired from the FPD in 2009 after 20 years of service. He now owns his own threat assessment consulting firm.

familiar rush of adrenaline that flows through your veins when the chase is on, and you know you are close. We were closing in on him, and we wasted no time.

Dusty, several patrol officers, and I drove straight to the house on Antoinette. We parked down the street for a safe and tactical approach. Cox had already killed one person that morning and could have been waiting to ambush the police when we came for him. The house was quiet, so I knocked on the door. After a few seconds, I heard footsteps and the door slowly opened. It was Cox's mother and stepfather. Cox was not there.

His stepfather explained that Cox came to live with them earlier that summer, but they'd kicked him out for not following the rules of the house. That afternoon, he and his wife came home and found Cox inside, along with a bike sitting outside the house they had never seen before. He also found a large caliber handgun in Cox's belongings. He was positive it was not a .22 caliber pistol but something larger, more like a .45 caliber. They told Cox to leave, which he did in a white cab. His mother thought he might have gone to his girlfriend's apartment across town at the Jillian Square apartment complex. Dusty called the Alaska Cab Company. There are only a few cab companies operating in Fairbanks, and at the time they were all using white vehicles. The dispatcher confirmed a cab had picked up a fare on Antoinette at 4:02 P.M. and terminated the ride at Jillian Square apartment B10. We were one step closer.

Our caravan of marked and unmarked patrol vehicles cruised across town to the Jillian Square Apartment complex. The complex is fairly large and encompasses several acres and several hundred apartments. We gathered around the door of apartment B10. I knocked very loudly several times with no response. I knocked again. Nothing. As we were walking down the hallway to leave, I told the guys we should set up surveillance on the place. Behind me I heard a door open. I looked over my shoulder and saw a female's head looking down the hall before quickly retreating inside. It was the door for apartment B10. Again I knocked loudly and told the woman to come to the door. After several tenuous minutes, the female opened the door and identified herself as Sarena Pinder[11].

Pinder acknowledged being Cox's girlfriend and that he had been at her apartment earlier that afternoon. She allowed us

---

11 This name has been changed.

into the apartment to confirm he was not there. We questioned her about her interaction with Cox, and she described it as nothing out of the ordinary while denying any knowledge of the shooting. When asked about Cox's whereabouts, she told us he might be at his friend's apartment in the University West neighborhood, but she could not be sure of the exact house. We left the apartment knowing she was not telling us the truth. We knew she knew more than she was letting on, but we didn't have anything to leverage against her.

We chose an apartment building at 211 Clarkson as our next house of interest. It was the most logical choice. The complex is outside the city limits, so I had never responded to calls there, but I had frequently overheard AST respond to the address over the years. It is a two-story building with apartments on both floors that all face to the west. There are no interior apartments. Dusty and I decided to start knocking on doors in the upper left portion of the complex and work our way to the bottom right. It was about 2:00 A.M. when we started waking people up.

Apartment #54 was the last apartment on the bottom floor. We could have just started there but no, we had to start on the top floor and work our way down. Dusty knocked on the door. The door opened about two inches, revealing an eyeball looking through the crack and the silhouette of someone beyond.

"Good evening. My name is Lt. Johnson with the Fairbanks Police Department. I'm sorry to bother you, but we are looking for someone who might be staying in the building. He is a short white male named David Cox. Do you know this person?"

"No," was the reply.

Dusty continued, "Okay, the guy has a tattoo on his arm." There was no response from the person behind the door. By this time I was tired and frustrated and tired of playing games with Little Dave all day long.

I said, "Hey man, the guy we are looking for has a tattoo on his arm that says 'Blood Money.' Can you just show us your arm to make sure it's not you, and we're outta here."

There was a slight hesitation and no response. Nothing was said, but in that moment, I knew we had our guy.

"It's him!" I said.

Before Dusty could block it with his foot, the door slammed shut. We backed off and called for more units. Minutes later officers from FPD, AST, the University Police Department, and the Airport Police arrived on scene. Some officers formed a perimeter around the building while others began evacuating other residents. We knew that Cox was armed and that he killed someone less than twenty-four hours ago, so we were not taking any chances.

When the building was surrounded, I yelled at Cox to, "Come out with your hands up." I realize that sounds a little cliché, but it sounded good at the time. More importantly, it worked. A few minutes later, Cox emerged from the house with his hands in the air. He was taken into custody without incident, and I escorted him to the nearest police car. I didn't ask him any questions at that time, but introduced myself to him and told him I would be speaking with him in a few minutes at the station. Officers secured the apartment to make sure no one else was inside. However, absent a search warrant, they could not search the apartment for any evidence related to the homicide. Once it was secured, the front door was closed and two officers remained on scene waiting for us to return with a search warrant.

I had been up almost twenty-four hours and was exhausted, but we finally had the shooter in our house now. It was time to catch my second wind, focus and get down to interviewing. I got a good look at the "Blood Money" tattoo when Cox was sitting in a chair in our interview room. It was hard to miss because it covered his whole right forearm. I guess he should have worn a long-sleeved shirt because that big tattoo sure made him easy to identify. He looked like a kid sitting there in the interview room. His baby face gave away his age, and although he was legally an adult, he looked maybe fifteen. I sat across from him with Dusty to my left across the table from him. I never liked having a table between me and a suspect. I wanted the ability to move into their personal space. I wanted to make them feel like I understood their motive, whatever it might be, for committing their crime. Sometimes you must get really personal to make that connection.

Cox had been detained, there was no getting around that, so before I questioned him I had to read him his Miranda warning. I pulled out my Miranda card, the same card I was issued back in the police academy and that I used for twenty years. It's faded and the edges are chipped, but you can still make out the familiar, "You have the right to remain silent…" I always read directly from the same card every time I Mirandize someone. I could recite the words in my sleep, but by reading from the card, defense attorneys will never be able to say I missed any of the phrases that must be communicated.

"David, I met you at the apartment, and I didn't really get a chance to introduce myself. I've been trying to call you all day today. My name is Peyton Merideth, and I am a detective with the Fairbanks Police Department. This is Dusty Johnson, and he is my lieutenant. I need to speak with you for a few minutes to try and get your side of the story on some stuff. One of the things we do is not make assumptions, but rather get the facts together about what happened to figure it out. This is your time to lay out for me and to hear your version of events about what happened."

Cox verbally waived his Miranda rights and agreed to speak with me. It is important to get a verbal waiver, especially if you are only audio recording the interview, as we were. If a suspect nods his head in an affirmative manner, that isn't recorded, so it's like it never happened. His attorney will say he never waived Miranda, and then it's your word against his, which in this day and age unfortunately isn't always good enough.

I began with, "Do you have any idea why you are here tonight?"

"No." His response was not unexpected, and I was ready for it. I figured he would play dumb for a few minutes at least. No big deal.

"I'll tell you what; let's just start at the beginning of your day. There was an incident that happened this morning, and I know you know what I'm talking about. There was incident that I know you were involved in." I was being careful not use the word murder. "I'm just going to lay it straight out for you from the start, because we are already starting out on the wrong foot. I've been working on this case since I got called at six o'clock this morning. I'm trying to get down to the bottom of what happened, and I'm trying to get all the facts, and I don't think I have them. You're the last person I need to talk to about what happened this morning. This is your chance to lay out for me what happened in your own words, your side of the story."

He responded, "I got up this morning at like six o'clock and went to work."

"Okay, did anything happen at work today?"

"I got fired."

"Why did you get fired?"

"I was sippin' bottles on the job. So I guess I'm in trouble for underage drinking." That was a pretty smart-ass response. He was pretty cocky, but then we were just getting started.

Cox continued to recount his activities after he had been fired, which of course, we knew was all a lie. He also said the night before he had slept at his "Booboo's place." Being a bit familiar with hip hop lingo, I knew he meant he had spent that night with his girlfriend. Dusty however, being twenty years my elder, had no idea what he meant. He had that, "What the hell did he just say?" look on his face.

The cat-and-mouse game continued for another ten minutes. Cox was going on and on about his day, and I interjected some questions here and there just to keep the conversation going and light-hearted. I wanted him to feel comfortable, but all the while he was just digging a big hole for himself. The more lies he told, the more lies he had to keep straight. I finally laid it out for him and fired a shot over the bow.

I asked him, "How old are you?"

"I'm eighteen."

"I'll tell you right now. Do you know how many eighteen-year-old kids I've sat right here and talked to that were sort of in the same spot you are in? Sitting in that chair, in this room talking to me? You're at a spot in your life where you aren't really sure what to tell me, and you're not telling me the truth so far." I paused for just a second to let that statement sink in.

I continued, "You are going to have to tell me the truth about what happened this morning. I've talked to five or six other people about what happened, but I'm still taking the time to sit here, after I've been up for twenty-four hours because I need to talk to you about it. You are the last person I need to talk to. I know what happened at the Carlson Center this morning, but I don't think I have all the facts about what happened because I haven't talked to you yet. This is your chance to tell me your side of the story."

He interjected a quick, "Well, I'm not lying," but it was a weak response, and I cut him off. Stopping the denials is a fundamental aspect of interviewing, and I was already tiring of this kid's lies.

"I have five or six people identifying you as being at the Carlson Center this morning. I have you dead cold being there...this is the only shot you get. This is a serious moment in your life, and I need your side of the story. You need to lay it out and tell me what happened..."

He responded, "Don't tell my girlfriend, but I was chilling with these girls, drinking...I left and got on my bike and started riding." Cox continued to describe how he met some guys in front of Lathrop High School and gave them some "chronic."[12] The guys called them later on and wanted meet to buy more marijuana. He was giving me pieces about what happened.

"I need to know what happened at the Carlson Center, David. That's where you met in the back of there, and that's where shit went down."

He said, "They didn't have the money and I dipped out."

Bingo. With that sentence, he at least put himself at the Carlson Center when the shooting occurred. He went there to sell Gary and his friends some weed, but they didn't have his money, so he left. Dusty had that curious look on his face again. I'm not sure he knew what "dipped out" meant. That dang hip hop lingo.

"So, you did meet them at the Carlson Center, yes or no?"

"Yes."

I continued, "So did you ride your bike back over to the Carlson Center?"

"Yes." Now we were getting somewhere.

"How many people were at the Carlson Center when you got there?"

His response, "Like ten of them." He was stretching the numbers a bit. My first thought was that he was already hinting at a self-defense claim. Here he was, a short little white kid about to be jumped by ten Native guys trying to rob him of his weed. I made a tactical decision and decided to give him a bite at the apple. If he bit on it he might have a good defense strategy in court. If not, he was screwing himself out of any possible defense.

Cox said, "They was all fighting with each other. That's why I didn't want to get in, cuz I figured they was trying to rob me. Dudes was looking all funny at me so I was like okay, whatever, ya'll don't have the money so I'm gone."

---

12 Chronic is a slang term for marijuana.

"Did you have a gun with you when you went to the Carlson Center?"

"No."

"Do you remember what you were wearing?" He described his red shirt and blue shorts and said he had a backpack. That was important, because not only did it match what the witnesses had described he was wearing, but I could put those clothing items on the search warrant for the apartment.

"Did you get into a fight with anyone?"

He said, "They looked like they was gonna rob me so why stick around." By denying he had been assaulted or threatened, Cox had put himself in quite the pickle. He denied shooting Gary of course, but as long as he put himself at the scene, that didn't matter. It's not very often you get even one eye witness to a murder, and in this case I had the luxury of having several.

After several more denials, I could tell that he was never going to budge off his story about not pulling the trigger, so I ended the interview. I was very pleased with our position and with the admissions we had elicited from him. With any luck, we would discover additional evidence when we served the warrant at the apartment.

It was 4:00 A.M. when Dusty called Detective Dave Elzey at home and told him to come back to work. I was at the courthouse securing the search warrant for the apartment. Dusty briefed Dave on how we had identified Cox and what had gone down during the interview. An hour later, we arrived at the apartment and began our search.

Under a coffee table in the living room, I found a neatly folded a red shirt and blue shorts along with a black backpack. Sitting right on top in plain view was David Cox's Florida ID. There was a red smear on the shorts that looked like blood. I remember thinking how cool that was and at the same time how dumb Cox had really been. If you keep the clothes you were wearing when you murdered someone, you might not want to leave your ID card sitting on top of them! I still use a photo I took of that evidence on scene in my academy death investigation class as an example of stupid things criminals do.

In a back bedroom sitting on a shelf was a .45 caliber handgun. This was the gun that Cox had in his backpack when he was fired from Chili's, and the same one seen by his stepfather not long after. Although we found some .22 caliber ammunition, we never found a .22 caliber pistol in the apartment. At the time, I guessed he had thrown it into the river. I suppose it is what I would have done. He was standing beside the river when he shot Gary, so the theory seemed logical.

By 7:00 A.M. I was nodding off at the District Attorney's Office writing a felony complaint, the charging document the judge would read later that afternoon at Cox's initial arraignment. At the time, Cox was officially charged with Murder in the Second Degree. I was so tired when we were done, I almost called Kristi to ask her to come pick me up. I stumbled in the house and spent a few minutes at the breakfast table with my family before heading to bed.

We had been running and gunning so hard that it wasn't until the following day I was able to sit down and have a long conversation with Gary's mother[13]. It was hard. She sounded so frail on the phone. I told her as many details about the case as I could. It was nice to be able to tell her that we'd caught her son's killer so fast. I promised to keep her updated and to sit down with her in person as soon we could.

An autopsy was performed a few days later at the State of Alaska Medical Examiner's Office in Anchorage. Gary had been shot three times in the head. With the autopsy report in hand, we easily pieced together what happened when we compared the results with the evidence we collected at the scene. Gary met with Cox on the bike path a few feet away from the rest of the group. When Gary told Cox he did not have the money to pay him, Cox pulled a gun. Gary turned to run and caught a bullet in the side of his head. The bullet traveled through his ear lobe, into his ear canal, and down into his jaw. The shot was not fatal, but Gary came out of his flip-flop, and he started to crawl on the ground away from Cox.

Based on the location of the spent casings, Cox circled around Gary and fired several shots at the group of kids that were now running away. The final two shots were fired into the back of Gary's head as he lay helpless on the ground. Execution style. Although he was initially arrested for Murder in the Second Degree, he was subsequently indicted for Murder in the First Degree based

---

13 To this day, I stay in touch with Gary's sweet mother. She still lives in Minto, AK, a small Athapaskan community in interior Alaska.

on the evidence showing that Gary was executed. All of this over a $40 bag of marijuana.

The case went to trial seven months later. Most homicide cases that make it to trial usually take well over a year to work through the court system. This case sailed right through. The assistant district attorney assigned to the case, Jeff O'Bryant, to his credit had refused to plead this case to a lesser charge. We were going to trial on the Murder in the First Degree charge, period. No plea deal for anything else. The case was just about as airtight as you could get. The red smear on Cox's shorts was identified through DNA testing as Gary's blood. After the first day of trial, Jeff, the assistant district attorney, suggested I go back and interview Pinder, Cox's girlfriend at the time of the shooting, one last time to see if she was ready to tell the truth about her interaction with Cox the night of the homicide.

She had moved to an apartment across town by then, but she was easy to find. I was surprised at how agreeable she was about speaking with me. Thankfully, Katrina had come to her senses and had moved on from her relationship with Cox. She told me that Cox had confided in her the night of the shooting that something had gone down and that he needed to leave the state.

"I have a letter from him," she told me.

"When did he write this? Is this something he mailed to you?"

"It was sent to me...he became friends with a guy in jail and when he got out he gave it to me," she replied.

She dug through a box in her bedroom and found the letter. As I read it, I tried my best to keep a straight face and act professional, like the letter wasn't that big of a deal. I thanked her and assured her that if she had to testify, everything would go smoothly. I drove straight to the District Attorney's office and showed Jeff the letter. He laughed. Then he had me run the letter over to Cox's defense attorney's office for discovery purposes. Discovery is the process in which all of police reports, photos, etc. are turned over to defense counsel prior to trial.

I took the stand the next day. Immediately following my introduction, Jeff asked me to read the letter. The defense attorney objected of course, but she was overruled by the judge. I think he was curious as well. I cleared my throat and took a drink of water, then I began to read. As a side note, the letter as detailed below is dictated as it was written and is not edited for grammatical or spelling errors.

What's Popin,

They might call you to the stand so heres your story... "David came home late. I figured he was out sell'in weed cause he pulled his gun out of his bag and put in his shoe. He got undressed and layed down. I dosed off till a call came on his cell. He got up and anserd. He said "How much you want? Yall gonna to pay for this one, okay I'm on my way." He put his shoes on and said he's be back. I'm sure he left his fun because I saw him leave I in his shoe. I didn't see him come home but I remember his gun was gone along with his work clothes. He came home told me he got fired from his job and if any cops came to tell them he didn't live there. After that he left to get a tattoo and I didn't see or talk to him.

David further broke the letter down into bullet points outlining possible questions Pinder might be asked on the stand and what her answer should be.

-What time did David come home that night? <u>Around 5:00 a.m.</u>

-What kind of gun was it? <u>A .45...he always braged about it.</u>

-Did he take his gun or did he left it? <u>He left it in his shoe but later it was gone.</u>

-Was he dealing drugs? <u>I know he sold week but that's all I know about.</u>

-Did he have a short temper? <u>He pouts but he's allways respectfull and calm.</u>

Any other Q's remember <u>YOU DON'T KNOW!</u>

At that point I took a long drink of water to pause for effect. Before I continued reading, I made eye contact with every juror sitting in the box. This was a time when I actually had fun sitting in court.

I'm sorry I drug you into all this drama. I'm a be real good when I get off. You probly gona laugh but Me an Jesus are getting closer everyday. And you better watch out 'cause I'm gona end up turn'in into your moma. But I just want you to know I'm crazy in love with you. I can't wait to get out but before we start back were we were at I want to give our relationship to Jesus. I'm not asking you to marry me...yet...but really love you and care about you.

Listen don't tell anyone about this letter and rip it up after you read it. Listen looney is forgiven for steeling my car and he and I have become close like bible buddies so treat him like family. If any one found out I gave you this story line I would be sure to be convicted so make sure you get rid of it. But if you can't remember write in your own words and keep that one. Don't even speak to me about the letter. Just know it and expect good things when I come home.

I love you,
David King

At first the "King" name through me for a loop, but it didn't matter. After I read the letter, Jeff led me through the investigation from start to finish. I was just getting to the part about finding Cox hiding in the apartment complex when his attorney asked for a recess and to speak to the judge in private. I knew what was coming. Ten minutes later, the attorneys and the judge emerged from a conference room. The jury was released, and just like that, the trial was over. I was still sitting in the witness box. Cox changed his plea to guilty of Murder in the First Degree and agreed to open sentencing. The outcome was the same as if the jury had found him guilty. The sentence was up to the judge.

I walked straight from the witness box to the gallery and gave Gary's mother a big hug. I had assured her the case was solid and there was a good chance for a conviction, but I was still relieved.

I whispered in her ear, "I told you everything was going to be okay." She cried on my shoulder and thanked me for all my hard work. I only hoped that the conclusion of the trial provided just a little closure for her and the rest of Gary's family.

One requirement included in Cox's plea deal was a stipulation that come spring, he had to show us where he disposed of the gun. On a sunny day the following May, Cox led our team to a wooded area behind the apartment complex on Clarkson. We had to use a metal detector to find the gun, but it didn't take long. Buried in the soil under a small birch tree was a .22 pistol with neon green sights. I had always figured the gun was thrown into the river. I still can't believe that those kids focused on and recalled the green sights on the gun. It was such a small detail in the scheme of things. They just focused on the threat. The barrel of the gun.

The Blood Money Homicide was officially closed. Cox was sentenced to 99 years with twenty-four years suspended. He could spend the next seventy-five years in prison over a $40 bag of weed. I just hope that he lost a little of his smart-ass cocky attitude because, well, he was kind of a little fella.

CHAPTER 5
TRISH

The 135-mile long Denali Highway winds its way through the foothills of the Alaska Range connecting the George Parks Highway to the west and the Richardson Highway to the east. Nestled along the Denali Highway, about fifty miles from the Denali Park entrance, amongst the towering peaks of the Alaska Range, is the Gracious Lodge. An Alaskan bush pilot and hunting guide named Butch Gratias opened the lodge in 1957. Married for nearly 40 years, Butch and his wife Carol have opened their doors to thousands of weary travelers, gold miners, hunters and adventure seekers from around the world during the short Alaska summers. Visitors have said the rustic lodge represents the real Alaska.

Within walking distance of the rear of the lodge there is a tall hill that overlooks the silt-laden Nenana River to the north and snow-capped mountain peaks in every direction. As a child, Butch and Carol's daughter, Trish, would play games and spend a lot of her time exploring the summit. It was her favorite spot amongst the vast wilderness that surrounds the lodge where she spent every summer. It's a beautiful place. Today there is a memorial on top of the hill that was built by hand from rocks pulled from the ground where Trish played as a child. There is a marker on top of the rocks that bears the inscription: In Memory Of Tricia L. Warren, 1976-1995.

During the last twenty years, or at least until I was promoted to detective in 2005, there were three unsolved homicides that people who live in and around Fairbanks spoke about with any frequency. Trish Warren was the first.

Trish was shot and killed on September 5, 1995 during a robbery at the Discount Truck Stop, a convenience store where she clerked. Only on the job for two weeks, she was alone that night, choosing to work the night shift because it paid an extra twenty-five cents an hour. At 4:09 A.M. an Alaska State Trooper walked into the store to purchase a newspaper and found Trish behind the counter. She had been shot twice in the forehead. Blood had trickled down her face and pooled on the floor. The cash register drawer was open and empty.

The fall semester at the University of Alaska began the first week of September 1995. I very was fortunate that I made it back to Fairbanks in time for my first class. For two weeks I had been working on the North Slope in a hunting camp for Clearwater Outdoor Services, owned and operated by my dear friend Pete Buist. There were five people in the sheep camp I had been assigned to, and we were scheduled to fly out in plenty of time for Pete's son, Jason, and me to get back to Fairbanks in time for school. Then some rough, fall weather came in hard and fast. The ceiling came down and it started snowing during my short Super Cub[14] flight out of the mountains to the base camp. I was so scared during the flight that after I climbed out from the cramped little plane, I literally kissed the ground. When I made it back to civilization, I read a headline about the murder in the **Fairbanks Daily News-Miner**. I recall thinking that the victim and I were about the same age.

The second memorable cold case happened on April 26, 2003, when the body of a young Alaska Native woman was found in a bathroom in the Bartlett Hall dormitory building on the UAF campus. Her name was Sophie Sergie. She had been shot and presumed to be sexually assaulted.[15]

The third happened on May 30, 1994, when a convenience store clerk name Barry McNulty was shot and killed during a robbery at the Garden Island Party Store in midtown Fairbanks.[16] Barry was a husband and father, whose wife still calls the investigations unit

---

14 The Super Cub is the workhorse plane in the Alaskan bush. It is known for its ability take off and land in short distances.

15 In 2019, Steven Downs was arrested by the Alaska State Troopers for the murder of Sophie Sergie. At the time of her death, Downs was an 18-year-old student at the University of Alaska living in the same building where her body was found. He is presumed innocent and is awaiting trial.

16 Barry McNulty's case has not been solved and is an active cold case investigation.

a couple of times a year hoping that progress has been made on his case. Several detectives over the years have reviewed the case, but no new leads have been developed, and unfortunately, the case remains unsolved.

By profiling these three cases, it is not my intention in any way to diminish the other unsolved murder cases still being investigated in Fairbanks, either by Fairbanks Police or the Alaska State Troopers. Murder cases are never closed until they are solved. However, these three cases seem to be the ones that people in the community remember. Perhaps it is because how these individuals chose to live their lives did not contribute to their deaths in any way. They were not participants in a drug deal gone bad, for example. They were innocent people going about their lives, working shifts and earning a meager salary to support their families. In the case of Sophie, she was just a college student living in the UAF dorms.

When I was promoted to detective in 2005, I inherited three cold murder cases. While I was excited to get to work, I was forced to choose which case to start with. I could only focus my efforts on one cold case at a time, so I picked the case that I felt was the most solvable. The first case was a double homicide that occurred in 1983 at an apartment not far from my parents' home. Two suspects had been identified, but the case never came together. The second was a burglary-turned-murder that occurred in south Fairbanks in 1985. It seems a couple burglars decided to end their partnership in crime after they stole a safe from a restaurant. One bad guy shot the other bad guy in the middle of Stacia Street and left the safe behind. There were no suspects. In my opinion it was the least solvable of the three cases.

The decision was easy. I dove head first into what had become known as the Discount Truck Stop (DTS) homicide. The victim was Tricia Louise Warren. I felt a connection with the case, maybe because Trish and I were the same age, or maybe I was intrigued because the murders of Trish Warren and Barry McNulty had shaken the community. People were still talking about the two convenience store clerks who had been killed within a relatively short time of one another. Although they were similar in circumstance, the two murders did not appear to be related.

I did not conduct the preliminary investigation, nor did I work the scene or have to touch the body of Trish Warren. My predecessors were tasked with that, and as always, did a fantastic job. They were just two or three pieces shy of solving the riddle. It was my job to solve an incomplete puzzle, glue it together so it would not fall apart and give her parents a reason to begin smiling once again.

This case became my life. I lived it and breathed it. In fact, amongst the few people who knew I was working on this book project, some went so far as to believe the entire book was about the tragedy that unfolded at the corner of Cushman and Van Horn on a crisp September morning in 1995. I understand why some would think that, because working the Trish Warren case had such a profound impact on my career and on my life.

Unlike the other homicide cases I have profiled, I struggled with how to properly present this case to the reader. The investigation into Trish's murder consumed me for nearly two years. A lifelong bond was forged between me and Trish's parents that will never be broken. They are now part of my family. I only hope that my writings about Trish, about how she died, and my pursuit of the truth do her justice. She deserves that and so does her family.

****

No fingerprints were found at the scene, not on the counter or on the cash register. The video surveillance unit didn't work, and none of the surrounding businesses had cameras aimed in the direction of the convenience store. No spent shell casings were found. Either the murder weapon was a revolver, or the suspect collected the casings before leaving. Only the body of a beautiful young woman lay on the floor behind the counter. The detectives checked the receipts from the register and from the gas pumps to determine approximately what time the last customer had come and gone. "No sale" was printed on the register receipt at 4:03 A.M., presumably from the suspect opening the till. Six minutes later at 4:09, the trooper arrived for his morning coffee and newspaper. Six minutes. Aside from videotaping and photographing the scene, there was not much else they could do.

Butch and Carol received the news that their youngest daughter had been murdered while they were in Anchorage on a quick fall shopping trip for the lodge. The call came from one of Trish's friends. Of course, they were devastated. They flew Butch's plane back to the lodge and traded the plane for a truck. Then they made the long drive to Fairbanks searching for answers.

Trish's husband, Russell Warren, was asleep in the barracks on Fort Richardson Army Base in Anchorage when he got the call about Trish's death. He was in Anchorage for a doctor's appointment. It was no secret among Trish's family and friends that she and her husband were not doing well. Like many young couples, they struggled with finances and the seemingly endless problems couples endure when they marry too young. They met when Trish was just seventeen, and soon after she became pregnant with the couple's first child. After Austin was born, she quickly became pregnant again, with another boy they named Dalton. The boys were ages one and two when their mom was murdered.

Ten years passed without an arrest being made in the case. It had been ten frustrating years for Trish's family waiting for answers that never came. Her family deserved a sense of closure. There were suspects, of course. Around the time Trish was murdered, a group of individuals were allegedly responsible for a rash of robberies around town. Using informants, detectives did everything they could to try and record these suspects talking about the recent robberies they had supposedly committed. If they happened to mention the Discount Truck Stop homicide, there would be probable cause to keep listening for specific details about the murder. One of the people they cued in on was a guy named Marvin Lamar Wright.

Unfortunately, the investigation stalled. The tips stopped trickling in. The case became cold. I can't blame the detectives who worked the case all those years for not making an arrest. That wouldn't be fair because they tried their hardest to solve a very difficult case. They played the hand they were dealt, and they played it well. Sometimes that's just how things work out. Murder cases are like puzzles, and some puzzles are bigger with more pieces and are more difficult to put together. When there are missing pieces, the puzzle doesn't fit together and it's usually placed on a shelf, sometimes for years collecting dust. It languishes untouched until someone turns over a couch cushion or moves a refrigerator and then bingo, they find the missing pieces. Then, they put the puzzle together. That is how cold cases are solved.

In February 2005, I removed a large dusty box containing the DTS case file from a shelf in our office. The contents had been picked over fairly well throughout the years, so nothing was really organized. There was a box of pictures and some three-ring binders full of reports and miscellaneous paperwork. Of course I was curious, so I looked at the photos before I dove into the police reports. The inside of the store was well photographed, paying particular attention to the area around Trish's body. There were photos of the outside showing the gas pumps and the parking lot. I looked at a photo of the sign and thought, *Really, gas was only ninety-five cents a gallon in 1995? Dang.*

Over the next few weeks, I organized the case into five three-inch, three-ring binders. I categorized all the police reports, laboratory reports, crime stoppers tip sheets and all the miscellaneous paperwork and notes that comprised the huge file. I hunted for an angle to start with, for where to begin.

One of the reasons I picked this case to work on was because Marvin Wright had been developed as a suspect early on the in the investigation. His name had been mentioned in a few crime stoppers reports. In 2003 a woman named Sherry[17], who at the time was incarcerated at the Fairbanks Correctional Center, told a guard that she wanted to speak with a detective about the case where the girl at the convenience store was shot. The detective who was assigned to the case went to speak with her. Sherry told the detective that Marvin Wright, aka Peanut, was the shooter. She also stated there were two other individuals there when the shooting occurred. Her version of events supported the assumptions of the original case detectives - that Wright was the individual who murdered Trish Warren.

Sherry was a long-time drug abuser and ran in the same circles with Wright around the time of the murder. However, there were parts of her story that didn't make sense, and in reality, she didn't mesh well with the detective who interviewed her in 2003. I am not attempting to place blame on why things didn't work out between them. They just didn't. Once again, hindsight makes it easy to cast blame. But I made the decision that approaching Sherry was the best way to begin my investigation. My hope was that because Sherry and I were about the same age, and that fact that I believe

---

17 This name has been changed.

I'm easy to talk to, I stood a good chance of developing a productive relationship with her.

She was easy to find because she was incarcerated at the Highland Mountain Correctional Facility just outside Anchorage in the community of Eagle River. Lucky for me, a close friend of mine was a sergeant at the facility. Maybe he could facilitate a friendly exchange? On June 20, 2005, I called Sherry.

"Hi, is this Sherry?"

"Yes."

"Hi, Sherry, my name is Peyton Merideth and I'm a detective with the Fairbanks Police Department. I know you spoke with another detective a few years ago about a murder case and well, that's why I am calling. I'm the new detective who was assigned to look into it. I was hoping to drive down there and speak to you about it again."

She had a bit of an attitude and was obviously surprised by my out-of-the-blue call. "I'm still worried about being charged as an accomplice because I didn't come forward sooner," she said.

"Sherry, all I can tell you is that if you tell me the truth, and you were not the one who pulled the trigger, you won't be charged with anything. I'll tell you what, do you know Sergeant Damron?"

"Yeah, he's cool as hell."

I chuckled. Gary is a great guy, but I had never thought of my buddy as being, "Cool as hell."

"Okay, good. He is a good friend of mine and can vouch for me okay? I'm a good guy and a straight shooter. If I drive down, will you talk to me?"

I was praying she would say yes.

"Sure, okay, I will talk to you."

"Okay, thank you. I will see you soon." With that phone, call my investigation into the murder of Trish Warren was officially underway. I was excited and hoped I had taken a small step in the right direction.

Six days later, I was sitting in a conference room at Highland Mountain Correctional Center face-to-face with Sherry. Although she had been around the block a few times with the police, we had never met. She was very anxious and looked really pissed just to be sitting there. Then again, I was pretty nervous too, so I'm sure from the outside looking in we made quite the pair. For the first thirty minutes or so we talked about her situation and the typical, "what can you do for me?" stuff that inmates always seem to want to discuss. I explained to her that I could not make her any promises, all I wanted was the truth about what happened and we would go from there. We finally got down to business.

"Okay, you get to the store, what happens? I mean, as far as who stays in the car, who goes in the store...it was you, Peanut, Cory, and Eric[18], right?"

Sherry had trouble making eye contact and she was picking her nails. She responded, "We were parked down here, away from the door, 'cause I was, we were smoking crack in the car. We parked away from the door so you couldn't see us. I was in the back seat, Cory was driving. Peanut was in the passenger seat, and I was directly behind him."

"Okay." It was a short response, but I wanted her to keep talking; she was on a roll.

"I handed Cory five bucks and told him I needed some fucking baking soda.[19] So I gave Cory the money, and I said I need baking soda to cook up some more...and I don't want to be prosecuted for that either."

People who do drugs are so paranoid. Here we are ten years removed from the night Trish was murdered, and Sherry was worried about being prosecuted for attempting to cook crack?

"So, who goes inside the store?"

"Cory, Cory goes inside. I told him I needed water and baking soda right...and I still have a little bit of water...some baking soda... Peanut is in the front, he's getting pissed at me, we are arguing back and forth over stupid shit, you know, and I was like 'What the fuck is taking him so long?' And then he (Peanut) goes, 'I'll go get him, I got this,' and so he went out. He got outside the car, and he went inside and then a few minutes went by, and I was like, 'What the fuck?' And then Eric gets out, and he goes inside, and I'm sitting there and like tick-tock, tick-tock."

"Seconds seem like minutes, right?" The more she talked, the more animated she became. I could tell she dreaded having to describe what happened next.

---

18 Cory and Eric's names have been changed.
19 Baking soda is common ingredient in crack cocaine.

There were tears in her eyes when she spoke next. "Right. Eric is in the bathroom. I came walking in, and I looked at Cory and I'm like, 'Where the F is my baking soda?' He was like, 'It's over here baby girl, come and get it yourself.' So I walked down the aisle, and I went and got it, and when I bent down to get the...I was back in the aisles somewhere, and knew when I bent down...and I heard Peanut say something to the girl, and the girl said something back, and he said something again, and I...it wasn't registering...I wasn't caring what he was saying, I wanted the baking soda...I wanted to cook some dope, and I...that sounds selfish."

"No, it wasn't." I knew I had to reassure her, keep her talking.

She nodded and continued. "And then I was like, 'So where is Eric?' And he was like, 'In the bathroom.' So I bent down to get the baking soda, and I come back up and hear...was looking sideways, I saw fucking Peanut grab a pistol out of his pouch...he was wearing like a brown or grayish down polar hoodie...and he pulls the pistol out and fucking went like this and you hear BOOM!...and...he shot her. My eyes got big...and I fucking started shaking."

Looking back, I think I was shaking too as Sherry described what happened after Peanut shot Trish.

"And I started shaking and had the baking soda, and I was shaking, and then Eric came running out of the fucking bathroom. And ahh...he looked at me, he looked at Peanut, and then Peanut looked over at me and saw how my face was. I must have had a fucked up look on my face."

"I'm sure you did. Keep going."

"And I started panicking and shaking, and it happened like... Cory was like, 'What the fuck man? What the fuck?' And Eric looked at me, and Peanut is looking at me, and he pointed the gun at me, and Eric stepped in front of it and said, 'I ain't gonna let you shoot my girl man, that's my girl,' and Peanut was like, 'Get outta my way, man!' And Eric was like, 'No, man, I ain't going to let you shoot, I ain't going to let you do that to her, I ain't going to let you shoot her, she fucking all right, she be all right.' And Peanut was like, 'Fuck that, this gonna come back and bite me in the ass, I'm getting rid of all evidence!' So Eric grabs me in a headlock, and he puts my head down in his chest, and he walks me out the door and...I kept thinking...he was going to shoot me in the back, and he gets me in the car and few minutes later they came running out."

All I could think at the time was, "Holy crap!" And it didn't stop there. Sherry went on to explain that they drove down South Cushman Street to the Tanana River and parked there for a while waiting for things to die down. Once again, Peanut threatened to kill her, but Eric intervened and kept her alive. We discussed the case for at least another hour. I pulled as many details from her as I could on the off chance she decided to never speak to me again.

I was pleased with the results at the conclusion of the interview. In fact, I didn't think things could have gone much better. I believed her. I really did. I tried hard to look past the drug abuse and the hard living. When convenience store clerks get shot at 4:00 A.M., stock brokers and bankers are not usually the witnesses. Paper boys, cab drivers, and druggies, those are your witnesses. Night people.

When I spoke with Sherry that day, I saw a young girl, just a kid really, who witnessed a horrible and traumatizing event. Trish and Sherry were about same age when Trish was murdered. Sherry was trying to do the right thing. I believed in her.

So I wanted to build on the momentum from the success of the interview with Sherry, to keep the pressure on. There was a reason why the case had gone cold, and I didn't want that to happen again. When I returned from Eagle River, our unit engaged in some serious round-table discussions about the direction of the case and what should happen next. I drew a diagram of the inside of the store on a whiteboard in the office showing where Sherry was standing when Trish was shot. I was really excited to tell the guys in the unit what I had learned. Some of them were skeptical about parts of Sherry's story, and they had every reason to feel that way. I couldn't blame them one bit, but what else did I have to go on? Ultimately, the decision on how to proceed was mine.

Detective Dave Elzey summed it up pretty well when he said, "Dude, I think she was there, no doubt about it. There's too much detail in her story for her not to have been. But you are going to need way more than that to get a conviction."

He was right. For starters, I needed another witness to corroborate Sherry's story.

I was given another vote of confidence by Lt. Dusty Johnson. "Peyton, this is your case. You do what you think is right and run with it. I'll support whatever decision you make."

I appreciated my boss's vote of confidence, but there was just one little catch; I was in limbo between being from investigator to detective. In February of 2005, I was assigned as an investigator with the unit, basically a "teaching or learning" position for patrol officers rotating through the investigations unit. Technically, I should not have been working on homicide cases at all, but since the Discount Truck Stop homicide was a cold case, no one really cared. I wasn't stepping on anyone's toes.

But during the summer of 2005, around the same time as my interview with Sherry, Detective Randy Coffey retired. His departure opened up a detective spot in the unit, something that doesn't come along very often. The promotional testing process was set for the middle of July, and the competition would be stiff for the coveted position. I had to prepare for the testing process, so the DTS investigation was going to have to be put on hold at least until August. I hated to shelve the case for even a week, but I had to concentrate on getting promoted so I could give it the time it deserved. If the job went to someone else, Trish's case would slip through my fingers and be assigned to the new detective. I wasn't about to let that happen.

The testing process was scheduled during the first week of July and would take an entire day to complete. The candidates were required to take a written exam in the morning, an exam based on a rather thick crime scene investigation book that we had to purchase ourselves. Talk about dry reading. There is nothing like reading a 400 page instructional manual to put you to sleep at night. In the afternoon, the candidates would be subject to a mock press conference and oral board.

I studied my butt off. When test day finally arrived, I felt very comfortable. I even came up with hypothetical oral board questions and wrote my answers down so I could rehearse my response. I admit, I was a bit anal about the process, but I wasn't going to fail for lack of preparation. I did fairly well on the written test. Most of the questions came straight out of the textbook. I made some mental notes about questions that I was not sure about and looked up the correct answers during our lunch break. I knew I missed a few, but not many.

Then we moved on to the oral portion of the test. I've never had much of a problem speaking in front of people, and my experiences on stage singing and acting have given me the confidence I need to stand up in front of a crowd. That attribute was helpful during the mock press conference and the oral board.

"Officer Merideth, please explain your understanding of the 4th Amendment of the United States Constitution."

Ha! One of the hypothetical questions I had rehearsed! "The 4th Amendment to the United States constitution protects citizens from unreasonable search and seizure. That includes their person, for instance when someone is placed under arrest, as well as their property. Essentially police officers are required to obtain search and arrest warrants because of the 4th Amendment."

"Officer Merideth, please explain how the Fairbanks Police Department Investigations Division should handle the investigation of cold homicide cases. How would you, as a detective, prioritize these cases?"

Are you kidding? I had been working on a cold case for a month straight! "Sir, cold cases are cold for a reason; they don't get worked on. These cases deserve special attention because going through one is very time consuming. I believe that one day a week, unless there are urgent cases pending, should be devoted to cold cases. Call it a cold case day."

Before I knew it, the oral board was over and the testing was complete. By the end of the day, I was exhausted but confident that I had done well.

Three weeks passed and nothing. Not a word on who got the promotion, and I was getting stressed. I was in the break room making lunch when one of the patrol lieutenants congratulated me on my promotion to detective.

"Where did you hear that?"

Obviously surprised, "Oh, you don't know yet?"

Five minutes later, I was summoned to Chief Hoffman's office.

"Peyton, here is a copy of the memo I'm about ready to send out department-wide. It was a close call."

Following a paragraph thanking all the applicants for testing and some more fluff about how the process was very competitive was a list of the candidates. My name was at the top!

"Thanks, Chief, I appreciate the opportunity very much."

"You've earned it, and I know you will do a great job."

On August 1, 2005, I was presented with my detective shield during a small ceremony in the Investigations Division. My father was able to attend, which was really neat. I'm sure my parents were happy that, at least for the time being, I wasn't going to be running and gunning on the street.

The first thing I did? I moved my stuff to a desk by the window. The view was much nicer on that side of the room.

                              ****

"Okay, Eric, think, think as best you can...take yourself back, Eric, just think and take a second. Take yourself back to that night because it's really important that we get all the facts straight. Where were you when you heard the shot?" I leaned in really close, so close I was practically sitting in Eric's lap. We had been going back and forth for nearly an hour, sort of a verbal judo sparring match between two guys each unwilling to give up an inch. I wasn't going to quit until the truth came out. So far he was winning.

I hadn't wasted any time getting back to work on the DTS homicide case. About a month after I earned my detective shield, I made arrangements for Eric to be transferred to Fairbanks from the Spring Creek Correctional Center in Seward, Alaska. I'm sure he was curious why he had been transferred until I sat down with him and brought up Trish's murder. He caught on real quick.

Eric had been around the block more than a few times. He had been in and out of the system most of his adult life, so he was accustomed to speaking with law enforcement officers. However, I could tell he was nervous. He remained very articulate, but nervous. It was clear that Eric knew deep down that, regardless of how many times he had been interviewed by the police over the years, this time it was different. I had Sherry's statement in my hip pocket so I knew what questions to ask. It had been ten long years since he walked into DTS with his friends Sherry, Cory and Marvin - ten years since he heard the shots and had seen the clerk slumped over, bleeding behind the counter. He had lived with the guilt of knowing what had happened for a decade...and it was time. I hoped.

"Like I said, I was over by the car, that's exactly where I was. I just know I responded to the situation when the gun went off."

Well, it was a start. We were finally getting somewhere. "Okay, well, just tell me what happened? What do you remember?"

"I seen, you know...him. I just seen her, shot, and him tripping out. He was threatening around, and I just say, you know, calm down and let's get out of here, you know...just calm down. I just knew that he did something foolish because he had believed that she had, you know, more money...it was mostly anger."

Eric was skipping his way through his thoughts, but I gave him the benefit of the doubt. He was telling the truth. It was just that he had never told this story to anyone before, and the words were not coming out right. His mouth was having a hard time catching up with what his mind wanted him to say.

"What did he say? I mean, did you see him going through the register or was he complaining?"

"Yeah, he was complaining that there was no money and stuff..."

"Okay, when you walked into the store did you see a gun?"

"He had a gun. Peanut had a gun."

"Did at any time you see Peanut or anybody else behind the counter?"

"I believe Peanut was behind the counter." The more he talked, the more he remembered. He began to paint a clear picture of what happened after Trish was shot. "I believe he began to threaten other people...he was like, he was like 'shut up!' The gun came back out and he was just really bugging out...you know what I'm saying? He was worried about somebody telling, and I was like...I was like... he was pointing the gun and stuff, and that's why I had to calm the situation down cause everybody was freaking out!"

One can only imagine the chaos that erupted inside the cramped store in the seconds following the murder. Druggies are paranoid enough. Throw four of them together with a gun at the scene of a murder, and you've got a circus. If the trooper had shown up just a few minutes before he did, things would have undoubtedly turned from bad to worse. Did Sherry and Eric know that Peanut was going to kill the clerk and rob the store? No, I don't think so, not based on what they had told me and more importantly *how* they told me. Everything had happened so quickly. They were both lucky to make it out alive.

My hopes were up, perhaps for the first time since taking on the daunting task of solving this case. Sherry's admissions had been a huge step in the right direction, but now, with Eric corroborating her story, the puzzle was coming together. That night, my wife Kristi and I went to dinner at Los Amigos, a Mexican restaurant on the Southside. Unable to help myself, I told her all about the interview with Eric. By this time, Kristi had a vested interest in the case because she knew how much solving the murder meant to me and to Trish's family.

"So, what's your next step? Where do you go from here?" she asked.

It was a great question. I had come up with several people who had spoken to detectives ten years ago who needed to be re-interviewed. And after going through old Crime Stoppers reports, I found a few people who had never been contacted by the police. One guy, another who I happened to go to high school with, called me from jail and told me that on the night of the murder, he had traded Peanut some crack for a bloody gun. The man had heard through the grapevine that I was investigating the case, and he wanted to get what he knew about the murder off his chest. He never even mentioned wanting a deal in return.

"I'm going to interview Peanut. He's next."

"Really? Where is he?" Kristi asked.

"California, baby."

****

Located about 175 miles North of Los Angeles, Federal Correctional Institution (FCI) Lompoc is a low security facility home to about 1500 federal inmates. The average resident is serving time for federal drug and or non-violent federal offenses. Inmate #13783-006 was Marvin Lamar Wright.

On May 11, 2000, Investigator Jim O'Malley (aka Jimbo)[20], who was assigned to the Statewide Drug Enforcement Unit in Fairbanks, received an anonymous tip that Wright and his girlfriend

---

20 Jim "Jimbo" O'Malley retired after 20 years of service with FPD. He is best known for his sense of humor and his work in the drug unit.

were staying at the Sophie Plaza Hotel. According to the source, they were supposedly checking out the next day. Wright had been on the unit's radar for allegedly selling cocaine in the Fairbanks area. He had several probation violation warrants for his arrest, and he was reported to be armed with a stolen handgun. Other investigators set up at the hotel that night, and although they didn't see Wright, they did spot a van that Wright was supposed to be using parked in front of the hotel.

The next day, Jimbo set up in the parking lot hoping to catch Wright coming from or going into the hotel. At about 9:15 A.M., Wright's van slowly pulled into the parking lot. A single black male exited the vehicle, looked around nervously, and then climbed over a railing and entered a room through the balcony door. A few minutes later, the same guy exited the room the same way he had entered, but he was carrying plastic bags full of clothes. Jimbo, using binoculars, recognized the male as Marvin Wright. He called for back-up.

On his next trip between the room and the van, Wright was taken into custody without incident. He didn't lie about who he was. The game was up, and he knew it. Officers found a bag of cocaine in his pocket and two handguns in the van. Cocaine packaged for distribution and handguns. It was a case tailored for federal court and an easy score for the U.S. Attorney's Office. Wright was eventually sentenced to serve nearly seventeen years in federal prison. In cop lingo he got "Federally fucked."

Lucky for me, Wright was serving his federal time in Lompoc, but not because federal prisons are easy to deal with, I always had to be escorted by an FBI agent. Lompoc is located just north of Santa Barbara, and I gotta admit, central California is a nice place for a cop from Alaska to visit during the middle of winter. I guess sometimes this job does have some nice perks.

I had plenty of time to think about what I was going to say to Wright during my leisurely drive up the Pacific Coast Highway between Santa Barbara and Lompoc. There wasn't a cloud in the sky, and the deep blue of the Pacific Ocean took my breath away. The setting and extra time to think gave me no illusions going into this interview.

In the back of my mind, I knew that Wright would never confess to killing Trish Warren. He had been around the block so many times that he knew the drill well. He had no reason to confess. I had no leverage to use against him, no smoking gun or new DNA results. This wasn't television. And this interview wasn't about a confession. It was about corroboration and nailing down as many facts as I could about Wright's relationship with Sherry and Eric.

The folks at the prison were neither helpful nor polite, which basically summed up my entire dealings with the prison from the get-go. Perhaps it was because I wasn't a federal agent, but a little professional courtesy goes a long way in my world, and I got none from the administration at Lompoc. I am convinced the people running the prison actually invented federal red tape, for holy moly did I have to cut through a lot of it during the months' long process setting up this interview.

In fact (a little note to the reader here), as I'm writing this, I'm on an airplane between Las Vegas and Seattle, and I'm so hot thinking about this topic I have to open my air vent. I would like to note that the way I was treated by these bureaucrats does not reflect my overall relationship with the feds over the years. I have had the pleasure of working with several hard working federal agents who care deeply about their country and the law. They are some of the finest law enforcement professionals I have worked with during my career. I won't name them here, but they know who they are.

The element of surprise was not on my side as I sat in the dingy, dilapidated office waiting for Wright to arrive. The windows were stained brown and were so dirty the bright sunlight barely shone through. Contrary to my repeated requests (more red tape), the administration demanded that Wright be informed that I had come all the way from Alaska to interview him about a case. In other words, they told him I was coming. Hmmm, I was guessing Wright knew which case. Seriously...what the hell is that all about? Why couldn't *I* tell him why I was there? I wanted to see the look on his face when I told him I was there to talk about an unsolved murder.

There is nothing like a first impression, and oftentimes, the look on a suspect's face says it all when you tell them why they are being interviewed. The prison officials were also concerned that this bumbling dumbass cop from Alaska would forget to read him his Miranda Warning, so they saw fit to take care of that little detail as well. Thanks, folks, that was a close one! I hadn't thought about doing that! And...who the hell is this Miranda person I keep hearing about?

So needless to say, Wright was fully informed and ready to go when he was finally escorted into the office. He sat down opposite me at the old wooden desk. His head was shaved, and he wore prison khakis with a long-sleeved, button-up shirt. Then there was the tear-drop tattoo below his eye.

I don't know how to properly document the next hour of my life or how to describe my interview with Wright, so I'm just going to start writing and see where my fingers take me.

He didn't confess to killing Trish, which I never expected him to do. But the interview wasn't pointless by any stretch. Not even close.

The first major hurdle was overcome when Wright agreed to speak with me at all. He at least agreed to hear what I had to say. If he didn't want to admit that he had shot Trish, that was fine with me, but by golly he was going to slip up somewhere and make some admissions that could be corroborated by other people. If I could keep him talking, I would at least accomplish that much.

It was like a chess match. Was Wright even in Fairbanks on September 5, 1995? Yes...whew! Got that minor detail out of the way right off the bat. Did Wright hang out with Sherry, Eric, and Cory about that time? Yep...and often. Good news. Had he ever been to the Discount Truck Stop with the three of them? Sure, all the time. More good news. All these little details were adding up. How about this one - had he ever traded a gun for drugs? More specifically from the guy in jail who had come forward. Yes. Now that was a big admission. He just didn't know that at the time.

Our conversation lasted about an hour until I was satisfied that there was nothing else to gain. The interview was about taking baby steps in the right direction. By themselves, they are pretty darn small, but when you add them up, you get somewhere pretty quick. I just hoped that the dominoes continued to fall in the right direction. I was playing the hand I was dealt, and so far I was beating the house. In the back of my mind, I believed the next time I saw Wright would be on the first day of jury selection.

****

Nearly two years passed before Wright saw the inside of a courtroom in Fairbanks. The team of prosecutors assigned to Trish's case fought hard in the months leading up to the trial. They fought and argued motions and court rulings and anything the defense threw at them. Then, they cranked up the fire and they fought harder during the trial. They fought for Trish and for Trish's elderly parents who sat through every minute of testimony. They fought for her two sons who grew up without their mom.

In the end it was Wright's mouth that got him into trouble. He just couldn't keep it shut. I ended up tracking down and interviewing several people to whom Wright admitted to over the years that he had killed Trish. Some of his confessions were boastful, some just off the cuff statements. But all that circumstantial evidence adds up. During their closing arguments, the defense argued that the prosecution was basically passing out deals to any inmate at the jail who was willing to make up a story and testify for the prosecution. The attorney even wrote the names of all of the witnesses who testified on a big piece of paper and left it on an easel in front of the jury so they could ponder over all the shady characters who had testified for the prosecution.

Then, when it was the prosecution's turn for the rebuttal closing[21], one of the prosecutors walked right up to the jury and said, paraphrasing, "The defense would have you believe, that Detective Merideth just ran through halls at the jail and yelled out, Let's make a deal!" Then he torn down the defense's list of names, wadded up the poster paper and threw it in the trash. Right in front of the jury. My jaw hit the table. The defense attorney started to say something, but he let it go. The judge was ready to say something, but because the defense attorney had kept quiet, what could he say? The moment was, well, indescribable.

It took only six hours of deliberation for the jury to return a guilty verdict against Wright for Murder in the First Degree and other lesser charges.[22]

Later that fall, the Gracias family put up a Christmas tree for the first time since Trish's murder.

---

21 During jury trials, closing arguments are first made by the prosecution, followed by the defense. Since the prosecution has the burden of proof, they get a short rebuttal closing after the defense.

22 Wright was sentenced to life in prison for the murder of Trish Warren. In 2010, his conviction was affirmed by the State of Alaska Court of Appeals.

The author poses with his family not long before his retirement from FPD

The junked car where Kaylynn Bishop's body was discovered
Photo courtesy of the Fairbanks Police Department

Kaylynn Bishop

Trish Warren
Photo courtesy of the Gratias family

FPD Investigations Unit during the winter of 2005
Left to right...Detectives Chris Nolan, Peyton
Merideth, Dave Elzey, Randy Coffey and Lt. Dave Kendrick.

The site where Daniel Fredrick's body was dumped near the Tanana River
Photo courtesy of the Fairbanks Police Department

Allen Brandt, killed in the line of duty on 10/28/16

A chilly, winter night on patrol in the Golden Heart City

*The author in 2004 sporting the City of Fairbanks
100 year centennial commemoration badge*

Wright convicted of murder in '95 slaying

By TIM MOWRY
tmowry@newsminer.com

A jury found Marvin Wright guilty Monday of murder in the 1995 killing of a convenience store clerk in South Fairbanks.

The jury needed only one day to reach its verdict after a four-week trial in which several of Wright's friends and associates implicated him in the murder of 19-year-old Tricia Warren at the Tesoro 7-Eleven Discount Truck Stop almost 12 years ago.

"Twelve long years," said Carol Rhoade-Gratias, Warren's mother, still sobbing outside the courtroom after the verdict. "I'm so happy for Tricia's little boys that today when I go home I can tell them 'guilty.'"

The jury of eight women and four men found Wright guilty of first- and second-degree murder, as well as robbery and tampering with evidence charges. Wright now faces life in prison. His sentencing is set for Feb. 7.

Dressed in a blue blazer, matching pants and a gray dress shirt, the 38-year-old Wright showed no emotion when the verdict was read by Superior Court Judge Niesje Steinkruger.

Warren, a mother of two young boys, was found dead by an Alaska State Trooper early on the morning of Sept. 5, 1995, after being shot twice in the head. The store's cash register was emptied.

The case went unsolved until a grand jury indicted Wright, a longtime suspect, on a murder charge. late in

> *"I'm so happy for Tricia's little boys that today when I go home I can tell them 'guilty.'"*
> — Carol Rhoade-Gratias

Sam Harrel/News-Miner
Butch Gratias, middle, holds his wife Carol Rhoade-Gratias, left, and daughter Tina Gratias outside the courtroom Monday where Marvin Wright was convicted of killing Gratias' daughter Tricia Warren during a robbery 12 years ago.

2005 after Fairbanks police re-opened the case. Wright was serving an 18-year sentence in federal prison on drugs and weapons convictions at the time of the indictment.

Fairbanks police detective Peyton Meredith, who was the officer responsible for re-opening the case, buried his face in his hands when the guilty verdict was read.

"I think that's what the evidence

Please see CONVICTION, Page A8

Sam Harrel/News-Miner
Marvin Wright looks over the gallery of the courtroom Monday before being convicted in the murder of Tricia Warren. Warren was killed in 1995 during a robbery of the convenience store where she worked.

*Front page story covering the conviction of Marvin Wright
for the murder of Trish Warren
Photo courtesy of the Fairbanks Daily News Miner*

Rookie officer at an indoor marijuana grow in North Pole in 1999
Note the muskrat hat

Digging through the rubble at the Geraghty Street fire in January 2014
Photo courtesy of the Fairbanks Daily News Miner

From college to the police academy to retirement, the author with close friend,
Lt. Greg Foster

*Deputy Chief Brad Johnson presenting the author with his
Detective badge during a promotion ceremony in 2005*

Author with a big bull moose

FPD Investigations Unit in 2012
Left to right – Dave Elzey, Dan Welborn, Chris Nolan and the author

Fairbanks winter scene   Todd Paris, Paris Photographics

The Carlson Center and the Blood Money crime scene where
Gary Titus was shot and killed by David Cox

The Discount Truck Stop on the morning of September 5, 1995

Blondies Antiques in downtown Fairbanks where Daniel Fredrick was murdered

Peyton Merideth

Department photo in 2004

CHAPTER 6
DEATH AT 40 BELOW

Interior Alaska is cold during the winter. I'm not really sure how else to describe the bitter cold, but an officer I worked with once said, "It chills your bones." People in the Lower 48 have a hard time with the concept that the temperature cut-off for students going to recess in Fairbanks is -20° F. I can recall school being cancelled for nearly a week when I was a kid because it was so cold—about -60°F. The only reason school was cancelled was because the ice fog was so thick that it was too dangerous for school buses to get around. However, just because it's cold outside doesn't mean police work stops or even slows down. The cold just presents challenges unique to policing in interior Alaska. I used to joke that during the winter people just kill each other inside.

Early in my career I responded to a call at a hotel near downtown after a woman who was on her way to a job interview with the manager, discovered a frozen body in a car in the parking lot. Seriously, this poor woman just happened to park right next to a car that had been sitting in the parking lot overnight, so the windows had iced over just enough that she could see this frozen dead guy with a hole in his head in the driver's seat. It was at least -40° F. As it turns out, FPD had been keeping an eye out for this guy for a couple days because we had received a report from the Anchorage Police Department that the man was suicidal and was driving to Fairbanks to kill himself. Why in the hell would you drive 360 miles to shoot yourself in a hotel parking lot in Fairbanks? I remember thinking there are plenty of places in Anchorage to check out nicer than this and certainly much warmer since Anchorage doesn't have the intense cold Fairbanks endures.

This guy was frozen solid and the revolver he had used to punch his ticket was still wrapped in his right hand. The engine company from the Fairbanks Fire Department showed up and confirmed that the frozen stiff was in fact dead. Now came the discussion about how to get him out of the car, which presented a whole set of challenges because the guy was frozen solid sitting upright in the driver's seat. A firefighter had the bright idea to tow the car to the police department garage to let him thaw out like a turkey. Not happening! Finally, we decided to cut the top of the car off and pull the guy out that way. Seemed like a good idea, but the firefighters wouldn't touch the car until the weapon had been secured.

I couldn't argue with that logic, so I did my best to pry the gun literally "from his cold dead hands" to quote a famous speech on gun rights. The officer behind me was laughing so hard because he couldn't wait to tell everyone else that Peyton got shot by a dead guy. Finally, I had to start breaking the guy's frozen fingers to the get gun out of his hand. I still remember the popping sounds from his knuckles cracking. And the woman who found the guy? Yeah, she did not interview for the job.

****

Dealing with frozen bodies was just something we dealt with all the time. Another guy decided to check out while laying up against a snow berm right on the side of a busy street in South Fairbanks. His weapon of choice was a 12 gauge shotgun. It was dark, bitter cold and snowing, so no one found the guy until the next morning.

Shooting yourself with a long barreled shotgun presents its own challenges, like not being able to reach the trigger if the barrel is under your chin. This guy had it figured out. He had cut a hole in his sock around the big toe on his right foot. It was so cold, we found him with his big toe frozen to the inside of the trigger guard. It was quite sad, that someone would want to end their life so badly that they would resort to this.

****

On a very, very cold December morning, Dave Elzey and I were called out for a "dead lady in the back of an ambulance." Why is there is a dead lady in the back of an ambulance? Why didn't they take her into the emergency room? Oh my God, did one of the paramedics finally kill some belligerent drunk and the ambulance is a crime scene? These were the questions as I drove to work at 4:00 A.M. on a bitterly cold morning.

As it turned out, the ambulance was an old, dilapidated ambulance left to rot on a piece of property in downtown Fairbanks. A transient had discovered the body of a middle-aged Alaska Native woman, naked except for a red sweatshirt wrapped around her neck. She was not even wearing socks, and she was frozen solid. If you tapped her leg, it sounded like knocking on wood. It was about -50° F, and it was so cold we could only take about ten photos before we had to warm up our camera.

Our initial thought was the woman had been sexually assaulted and strangled. It was a logical conclusion based on the scene. There were empty alcohol bottles strewn about, she was naked, and the shirt was wrapped around her neck. However, without an autopsy there is no way to make that determination. I'm not a doctor and standing in the back of this rotted-out ambulance freezing our asses off, we just wanted some hot coffee and a warm office. But what if the case turns out to be a homicide? What about the scene? Well, the scene was technically on wheels, so I had the funeral home come pick up the body for transport to the medical examiner's office, and I called a tow truck for the ambulance. We literally towed the crime scene to the impound lot. That was the best idea I could come up with.

As it turns out, the woman died of hypothermia and had stripped herself naked just prior to her death. It made sense because there was no evidence of trauma. She had probably pulled her shirt up to wrap it around her ears. Studies show that prior to freezing to death, your body goes through a state of euphoria and the blood rushes out of your extremities to warm vital organs. This causes the victim to feel hot, so they strip off their clothes. This was an extreme case. It was -50° F and this poor woman had even taken off her socks.

****

It was March, 2007 and it was about -30° F when Dave Elzey and I were called out to what turned out to be one of the most brutal homicide scenes we had witnessed...and we have seen a lot. The case wasn't a "who dun it" because the suspect, an insane psychopath, was already in custody and talking about the little green aliens that made him do it. The murder occurred in the deep snow outside of a mental health assisted living facility in South Fairbanks. The victim, a beautiful young girl, was the only person working that night when she asked the suspect to cut a telephone call short so another client could use the phone. He freaked out and chased her out a side door and into the deep snow.

There is no other way to put it. On her 32nd birthday, this poor young woman fought for her life in the deep snow at -30° F until this crazy guy got around behind her and just about cut her head off. In fact, the force he used was so strong he broke the blade of the knife. She had deep cuts on her forearms and hands, defensive wounds that she received grabbing for the blade trying to fight him off.

It was one of those scenes that still haunts me. I think if she had run out the front door she may have outrun him, but the snow on the side of building was too deep, and it slowed her escape. Staring at her body there was no way not to put yourself in her position. How many times had I fought with suspects in the snow and made it out unscathed? Fighting in the snow is hard. That is why police train for fighting in the snow - because it is physically exhausting. But this poor girl just didn't have a chance. It was absolutely brutal.

After he murdered her, he ran across the parking lot to his room where he was later arrested by the FPD SWAT team.[23]

---

23 After four years of legal wrangling over his competency, Brian Galbraith eventually pled guilty to Murder and was sentenced to at least 20 years in prison.

CHAPTER 7
DANIEL

When I was kid I used to ride my bike from our home in Hamilton Acres to The Comic Shop which was in the middle of downtown. My friends and I were always trying to improve our travel time by finding new routes through the maze of downtown streets. We never crossed the busy Steese Highway, something my parents constantly worried about because we circled under the busy thoroughfare on the sidewalk next to the river and then walked our bikes up the steep steps to the bike path on top of the bridge on the other side. We often stopped to look at the graffiti spray-painted under the bridge. Some of the same artwork is still there today. I laughed at the guys who had spray painted hearts around some girl's name. What a dork. Why would you love a girl? Girls weren't cool. Baseball and WWF wrestling was cool.

In those days The Comic Shop was like a library for kids where you didn't have to be quiet. They sold comic books and baseball cards. I love baseball cards. My buddies and I would spend hours in the store going through boxes of cards picking out our favorite players and hoping that we didn't already have the card we wanted to buy. We didn't want duplicate cards. That was a waste of our allowance. I got into the comic book scene a little bit, but it was the baseball cards that intrigued me the most.

The Comic Shop changed ownership and locations several times over the years. They don't sell baseball cards and comic books any longer, but now sell role-playing games and fantasy books. Times have changed.

One day my friend Brett and I were riding home from The Comic Shop when we chose a new route that took us by the intersection of Lacey Street and 7th Avenue. There was a store on the corner called Blondie's Antiques. I had never been in the place, but I saw something in the window that grabbed my undivided attention. Inside a display case was a sheet of old baseball cards. We dropped our bikes on the sidewalk and went into the store. No doubt the owner, who seemed nice enough, was skeptical about a couple of twelve-year-old kids in his shop.

Having never been accused of being shy I asked, "Sir, do you sell baseball cards? I saw some in the window."

"Well, yes, I sure do. But, the cards I sell are very old and expensive. I don't think you can afford them."

"Could I still see them?" I knew I couldn't afford them, but I still wanted to see what neat cards this guy had.

The man walked in the back and emerged a couple minutes later carrying two three-ring binders. He sat down at a table with us. I opened the first binder and was amazed at what I saw. As I slowly flipped through the pages my eyes widened and my grin got wider. Mickey Mantle, Warren Spahn, Hank Aaron, Eddie Mathews, Willie Mays...they were all there. It was awesome. I never took the cards out of the sleeves but for a baseball nut like me, even as a kid, I was speechless. Just looking at rare cards like that in person is so cool. And no, the man wasn't kidding when he said I couldn't afford the cards he sold in his antique store—I still can't afford them!

I visited Blondie's often after I discovered the treasure trove of baseball cards that day in his little downtown shop. The man with the goofy, comb-over blond hair was always patient, even with an annoying kid bugging him every Saturday asking to look at his baseball cards. He was always nice. I always wondered if he was wearing a wig or if that was his real hair.

His name was Daniel Fredrick. Twenty years would pass before I found his frozen body dumped along the Tanana River in South Fairbanks.

****

I was not working the day Daniel Fredrick was reported missing, on December 19th, 2008. It was a Friday, and I was scheduled to be on call that weekend beginning at 5:00 p.m. I had enjoyed my day off from work, spending most of the afternoon Christmas shopping. On my way home I stopped by the station to grab something I had forgotten on my desk when I ran into Detectives Chris Nolan and Dave Elzey walking out the door.

"Hey, you are on call this weekend right?"

"Yep, sure am. What's up?" I asked.

Chris replied, "Patrol just took a missing person report on Daniel Fredrick, the guy that owns Blondie's Antiques. We are headed over there to see if anything looks suspicious. I just wanted you to know in case you get called about it later."

"Ok, no problem. Let me know if you need anything before then." I drove home and didn't think much about the conversation. If they needed help either Chris or Dave would call but more than likely the report would be on my desk first thing Monday morning if Daniel didn't show up by then. I wrapped some Christmas presents and was just sitting down to dinner when the phone rang.

"Peyton, hey, this is Jeremy. Adams is working a missing person case, not sure if you heard about it yet. I think we are at a point where we need a detective to come in. Chris and Dave already went home for the day." The call was from Sgt. Jeremy Lindhag and the officer he was referring to was Officer Ace Adams.

"Ok, no problem. I'll be there in just a bit." When I left that night, I didn't know whether I would be home in a couple hours or a couple days.

Officers Adams and Welborn had responded to the antique store after a friend of Daniel's called the police because he hadn't seen him in about a week. The strange thing was Daniel's dog was inside and Daniel never left for an extended period of time without his dog. They also observed a lot of dog feces on the floor which is never a good sign. After they arrived, the officers were contacted by several other concerned neighbors and friends who noticed the police cars parked out front. None of them had seen Daniel for several days.

Several other things seemed strange. The original caller walked through the residence with the officers and noticed that although the home was usually in some state of disarray several items were out of place. Newspapers had been left in the paper box that dated back over a week. They noticed a calendar hanging in the living room. Several days on the calendar were circled, including the 19th, and there was what appeared to be a to-do list found nearby. The word "passport" was an item noted on the list. Did Daniel leave town for Christmas? Perhaps he took off and his dog sitter had forgotten to stop by? The officers and detectives were left with more questions than answers when they left the residence that evening. One of Daniel's friends agreed to take care of the dog so that was one less thing to worry about.

After returning to the station, Officer Adams continued to work on the case. He started digging into Daniel's personal finances to see if his credit or ATM cards had been used recently. They had been. He contacted a security officer for Wells Fargo and determined that Daniel's Wells Fargo ATM card had been used to make numerous withdrawals at several locations around town. The bank card associated with his other business, Blondie's Military Supplies, had also been used. The activity was too suspicious not to raise a red flag. There were just too many withdrawals from too many locations in a short amount of time.

A significant purchase had been made at the AT&T store using Daniel's credit card that morning at 9:40 a.m. Officer Adams contacted the branch manager who confirmed that an individual named Raymond Jones had used the credit card to purchase a new 8GB Apple iPhone. Although Jones' name did not match the name on the credit card he used they allowed him to make the purchase because he showed them his Idaho driver's license. It didn't make any sense why they let him use someone else's credit card, but they had. Then Officer Adams told me the good news.

"Get this Peyton. This Jones guy added the iPhone to his existing AT&T account! That's how we know without a doubt that he is the guy who used Daniel's credit card! Can you believe that?"

I replied, "Not really! Good work. I can't believe this guy could be so stupid. What address do they have listed on his account?"

"1166 Vincent Court in North Pole. I ran him through APSIN (Alaska Public Safety Information Network) and it shows he has an address on Fort Wainwright, so I'm guessing he's in the military."

"Ok, good deal. I'll get to work on this and contact CID and see what they can come up with. Maybe they can confirm if the address on base is correct. If it's not, I will get to work on a search warrant for the Vincent Court address."

I knew that no matter which address proved to be the correct one I had some typing to do before we could do anything. I made a phone call to my contact, Special Agent Eric McKinley, at the Army Criminal Investigation Division office.

"Eric, hey buddy this is Peyton, what's going on?" Eric was a friendly guy and a great military resource. We had worked together many times before.

"Same 'ol, what's up?"

"I need a couple things. First, can you tell me if Raymond Jones is listed as a soldier on the ALPHA roster on Fort Wainwright. Second, can you confirm what address you have for him? APSIN shows an address in the barracks on Gaffney but I have information he may be living off base."

"Yea, sure thing but can you tell me what's going on? I have to tell my boss something."

"Well right now we have a missing person case and apparently this Jones guy has been using our missing guy's credit card around town."

"No problem. Give me a few and I'll call you back."

I got to work on the search warrant for the Vincent Court address. I was pretty specific when detailing what items we were searching for on the warrant. The list included Daniel's credit cards, ATM cards, the iPhone and a list of receipts from purchases that had been made using the stolen credit cards from several locations including Walmart and American Eagle clothing store. We didn't know what items had been bought but whoever made the purchases may have kept the receipts.

I got call back from S.A. McKinley. "Hey Peyton, the address in the barracks is no good. I will keep working on it but right now your intel on the North pole address seems the most current."

"Ok, thanks Eric. Keep digging and let me know if you come up with anything else."

It was almost 10:00 p.m. by the time the judge signed off on my warrant. We drove out to 1166 Vincent Court in North Pole. Our team consisted of Detective Dave Elzey, my good friends from the Alaska State Troopers Sgt. Jeremy Rupe and Mark Eldridge and me. More times than not the address listed on cell phone contracts is current so there was a good chance Jones was inside as we made our approach. We positioned our team around the house and Detective Elzey and I walked up to the door. I knocked softly.

The door was answered by a friendly woman who told us that Jones no longer lived there. He used to but moved out a few months ago. She used to baby sit Jones' daughter. Unfortunately, she did not know where he was living nor did she have a good phone number for him (we had the iPhone number but didn't want to call it right away to spook him). For some reason she thought he was possibly living off Chena Pump Road somewhere. As we walked away, I prayed that she was telling us the truth and that she wasn't calling to warn Jones the police were looking for him. In 2008 the technology was not readily available to triangulate cell phone signals. We were going to have to find Jones the old-fashioned way.

There was nothing else we could do for the time being but in my gut, I knew something wasn't right. I can see this Jones guy and probably a couple buddies breaking into Daniel's place and stealing his credit cards or maybe even stealing them out of his mail. That happens around town all the time. The problem was the dog. Why had the dog been left in the house alone long enough that he had defecated several times on the floor? That is what bothered me the most, the darn dog.

****

The night that Daniel Fredrick was reported missing, I didn't sleep well. Deep down, I knew there was a better than average chance that Daniel was dead. The dang dog still bugged me.

Life never stops, even during ongoing investigations. I made breakfast for Kristi and the boys, but I knew I was just a phone call away from returning to work. The call from Special Agent Eric McKinley came at 10:00 A.M.

"Good morning, Peyton, I think I have some good news for you."

I was excited. "Whatcha got, Eric?"

"Well, I didn't get the message until this morning, but last night Jones's commanding officer left me a voicemail. Jones is living at 1421 Kent Court, apartment A."

"That makes sense. Kent Court is in the University West neighborhood off Chena Pump Road. Thanks, Eric. I'll keep you posted."

It was the Saturday before Christmas, and here I was called back into work on my day off. My boys were at the perfect age for enjoying everything the Christmas season brings. They were counting the days until Santa came to our house. I kissed them goodbye and told them I would be home as soon as I could. My only consolation was that at least I was making some overtime to pay for all the presents I had bought.

Before meeting the other detectives at the station, I drove by the address on Kent Court. It was hard to tell because the parking lot was full, but there appeared to be three vehicles parked in front of apartment A. They included a white Ford Ranger, a sportier Ford Ranger Splash and a small blue sports car of some kind. I drove back to FPD and met with Chris and Dave, and together we decided they would do surveillance on the apartment while I obtained a search warrant.

By the time they drove back and got set up on the apartment, the white Ford Ranger was gone. Not long afterward, someone emerged from the apartment and drove off in the Ford Ranger Splash. Dave continued to watch the apartment while Chris pulled in behind the Ranger. Once the Ranger had traveled a good distance from the apartment, Chris called a patrol unit to have the truck pulled over. I was still at the station typing the search warrant, but I was monitoring the radio traffic. The driver of the truck was identified as Brian Towndrow. Towndrow...Towndrow...now that name sounded familiar, but I couldn't place it right away. Then I remembered.

Back in April, I had investigated Towndrow after his fifteen-year-old sister-in-law reported that he had sexually assaulted her. I worked the case, which resulted in Towndrow being arrested for Sexual Abuse of a Minor in the Third Degree and Sexual Assault in the Second Degree. He was in the military at the time but was discharged after he was incarcerated. Obviously, whatever plea deal he cut must have been a good one because he was already out of prison. Chris had the Ford Ranger impounded with instructions that it be towed to FPD. Towndrow was detained and also brought back to FPD for questioning.

With the search warrant completed and signed, I drove to the apartment to meet Dave and Investigator Eldridge. The only vehicle left in front of the apartment was the blue sports car, a Subaru Impreza and it was running. I didn't recognize the name on the registration. Warrant in hand, I knocked on the door, and it was promptly answered by a man I assumed to be Raymond Jones.

"Hi, are you Raymond?"

"Yes."

"I'm Detective Merideth with the Fairbanks Police Department. This is Detective Elzey and Investigator Eldridge with the Alaska State Troopers. We would like to speak with you for just a moment."

He shrugged as he responded, "Sure."

We filed into the apartment. Jones, his toddler-aged daughter, and another man named Michael Moore were all inside. While we had a warrant to search the apartment and we could have just barged in, that sort of entry would not serve any purpose. I wanted these guys to stay calm and talk to us. I presumed Daniel's body was somewhere out there, and without one of these guys talking, we would never be able to find him.

Dave and I spoke to Jones in the living room away from Moore, who was talking with Investigator Eldridge. I immediately noticed an iPhone lying on the floor near the couch and what appeared to be a brand new Sony television mounted on the wall. It was my assumption the television had been purchased at Walmart.

I repeated my usual introduction to him and jumped into the interview. "I'm sorry for the intrusion, but your name popped up in an investigation, and I need to speak with you about that for a few minutes. I just need your cooperation and some honesty."

His hands were shaking. "Okay."

"Obviously, you are not in handcuffs and you are not under arrest right now, but I am going to read you your rights. I'm going to do that because we came in here and startled you and because there are other officers in your apartment."

This was a tactical decision. Technically, Raymond could have been free to leave the apartment even though we were there to serve a search warrant. However, if he made any incriminating statements during the interview, I wanted the option to detain him. If I had told him from the start that he was free to leave and then later detained him I ran the risk of losing all of his statements because he had not been read his rights. I was erring on the side of caution and hoping he would not request an attorney.

I read him his Miranda Warning from the same old battered card I was issued in the academy. He verbally waived his rights and agreed to speak with us.

I started with a bit of small talk. "That is a nice TV, by the way. Where did you get that?"

"That's my buddy's, Brian Towndrow."

"Do you know where he got it from?"

"I have no idea."

Lie number one.

I didn't beat around the bush very long. "Do you have any idea about why we need to speak with you today? I'll tell you right now, Raymond, we have been working on this case for a couple days, so this isn't just by chance that we happened to come into your house today. Like I told you before, honesty is going to go a long way with us and make things a whole lot easier. There are probably some things that are easy to explain and some things that aren't, but we need to get down to the bottom of this. Do you have any idea why we need to speak to you?"

"No, sir."

"Do you have a cell phone?"

"Yes, sir."

"What kind?"

"It's an iPhone."

"When did you get the iPhone?" I specifically phrased the questioned that way so he could not say that someone else purchased it for him.

"A couple days ago."

"What store do you normally shop at? I mean, who is your account through?"

"AT&T."

He was already painting himself into a corner and I felt a surge of victory at his missteps.

"What's going on, Raymond, is that there have been some bank cards and check cards that belong to an individual which have been used around town. There is a considerable amount of evidence that you and some others have been using these cards around town buying stuff with them. I'm not going to beat around the bush a whole lot with you here, because honestly, this is a closed case. We already have a lot of evidence. I know about the iPhone and that it is on your account and how it was paid for. Do you still have these cards?" I fired that shot over the bow and didn't even ask if he had done it. He already knew we had him.

"No sir."

"Where are they now?"

"I don't know, they got tossed."

"Who tossed them?"

"Brian did."

Now we were getting somewhere. During the next twenty minutes, Jones admitted that he had used Daniel's credit cards to make several purchases around town. He denied using the cards to make any ATM withdrawals. Jones also stated that Brian Towndrow had provided the cards to him and Michael Moore a few days ago, and that he did not know how Brian had obtained the cards. Jones and Moore used one of the cards to buy some movies and a laptop computer from Fred Meyer. He was also present when the big Sony television was purchased at Walmart.

We discovered the blue Subaru Impreza belonged to a soldier who was currently deployed in Iraq. According to Jones, they had been using the car. Located in the ash tray was a Fred Meyer receipt for a purchase made on 12/18/2008 for $147.96. Receipts were listed on our search warrant as items we could seize. There were two bank cards found in the center console with the name Daniel Fredrick on them. These were the two cards that had been used around town the most. Both were Wells Fargo Visa check cards.

In the living room, we found a Walmart bag that contained a receipt for a purchase made on 12/18/2008 for $1627.84, the amount of the Sony television. In the same bag, for some reason, was a Fred Meyer receipt in the amount of $924.91. Jones and Moore stated that purchase covered the laptop computer and a bunch of DVDs that were scattered around the living room. All of the items, including the television, were seized as evidence.

While we were searching the apartment, Brian Towndrow's wife drove up in the other white Ford Ranger that had initially been parked in front of the apartment. Dave noticed a pair of snowshoes with the price tag still on them in the bed of the truck. He also recognized the price tag and the handwriting, as being similar to the price tags on other items for sale inside Blondie's Antiques.

Jones and Moore were both transported back to FPD for further questioning. Chris had already conducted an interview with Towndrow, but during subsequent interviews that afternoon, none of the three changed their stories. Both Jones and Moore stated they got the cards from Towndrow. Towndrow was saying he got the cards from Jones.

Although I could have easily obtained a warrant, Jones made that unnecessary by consenting to having his Ford Ranger searched. Inside the truck was a small white piece of paper found inside of a shoe on the back seat. Written on the piece of paper were the name Daniel Fredrick and an account number. The account number corresponded to Fredrick's business account at Wells Fargo. My guess was the piece of paper had fallen out of Fredrick's wallet. I'm not sure how the paper wound up inside of a shoe. We also found paperwork for a storage unit from Hide-a-Way Storage, unit F2.

We were in a tough spot. All three of our suspects had admitted to using Daniel's credit cards and knowing they were stolen. That was easy to prove with the mountain of evidence we had collected. While that was all well and good, we remained concerned about Daniel Fredrick's whereabouts.

We made the decision to arrest all three on several counts of Fraudulent Use of an Access Device. We still had more questions than answers. My hope was that after spending a night or two in jail, one of the three would decide to play "Let's Make a Deal" and tell the truth about what happened to Daniel Fredrick.

****

It had been nine months since I had sat face to face with Brian Towndrow, although the setting during our first encounter was a bit less dramatic and dreary. We first met when we spoke about the sexual abuse allegations made by his young sister-in-law at the building where his infantry unit worked on Fort Wainwright. That time he had confessed and was arrested later that day. I still couldn't believe he had gotten out of jail so quickly.

We sat across from each other in an attorney/client room at the Fairbanks Correctional Center. This time, instead of camouflage military fatigues, Towndrow sported a yellow jump suit.

It was 4:45 P.M. on the afternoon of December 21st when I met with Towndrow regarding Daniel's case. Earlier that day he had told a correctional officer that he wanted to talk to a detective. That message eventually flowed downhill to me. We had figured right. It only took twenty-four hours for one of the three suspects in Daniel's disappearance to break down and want to talk about what really happened.

Brian immediately requested that his attorney and the district attorney be present when he gave a statement. This caught me off guard, but I rolled with the punches as best I could. It was late on a Sunday afternoon. I didn't want to wait until Monday morning to make his request happen, but logistically this was a pain in the ass.

"Okay, Brian, let me make a couple phone calls then. But if I'm calling the DA on Sunday night and other attorneys...I mean...are we talking about the missing guy are we talking about credit cards?"

He was quick to responded, "This is about what is going on with the whole case."

I knew I couldn't use that statement in court since he'd already requested an attorney, but I was not about to waste my time and the time of the attorneys the weekend before Christmas to talk more about stolen credit cards. Based on the way he answered my question, I knew he was ready to talk about a lot more. So I made the calls and got lucky. Both the on-call district attorney and Brian's attorney answered on the first ring. I explained to them the urgency of the situation, and they agreed to come straight to the jail. I was impressed.

Towndrow, his attorney, and the district attorney worked out an agreement in exchange for his cooperation. I wasn't in the room when the three of them spoke, but when I returned, both of the attorneys reminded him that he had to tell the truth about everything or he could lose his deal.

"Okay, to start at the beginning, about the time I got out (of the military) Jones and Moore got involved with snatching some MREs[24] from work. No one is exactly sure how many they took and sold to the Blondie's military store, but the military was charging them with over two hundred counts. A week or so before I got out of the Army, it all blew up in their faces about the MREs. They went to a storage unit and unloaded a bunch of MREs. I was in the back of the truck stacking MREs."

According to Towndrow, the commanding officer of the unit didn't care how the MREs were returned or who took them, he just wanted them back. The storage unit Towndrow was referring to was owned by Daniel Fredrick. A few days before Daniel went missing, he reported that his storage unit, at Steese Mini Storage, had been broken into.

Growing more confident in his words, Towndrow continued, "A couple days later Jones and Moore are freaking out. Come to find

---

24 Meals ready to eat (MRE) are common military rations.

out later on, this was not just any old storage unit they opened up and taken stuff out of. It turned out to be the storage unit owned by Blondie's."

Towndrow went on to explain that Jones and Moore were freaking out because they believed that they were still under investigation for not only stealing the MREs but also other military equipment they had taken from Daniel's storage unit, equipment they had stolen from the military and sold to Daniel.

"They asked me to give them a ride because Jones's truck was in the shop. They asked me to give them a ride over to Blondie's. I parked in the parking lot next to it. They had talked to Blondie, they had talked to him about whatever, and they called him up...and talked to him about a bunch of gear that had been stolen and sold and that CID was watching them and watching the store and they had to make sure everything was out of the store to keep everyone out of trouble.

"They went in and a while later, they were like 'pull around front and pick us up'...I pull in they threw a bunch of stuff in the back of the truck. So we drive off and they were like 'well we need to get rid of some of this stuff.' So, they had me drive out to the flats and start throwing stuff out. They were like, 'don't say anything about this stuff because it's gonna be bad if you say anything.' They were dumping some equipment and they pulled a sleeping bag out of the back of my truck. At that point I was out of the truck to help toss some shit away because I was freaking out because they had just stole some stuff. Well, they pull the sleeping bag out, and there is a face in the sleeping bag. At this point I'm really starting to freak out and that's when they informed me that 'if you say anything you will be dead and your children will be dead as well.' They dragged him off into the woods and came back said, 'okay, let's get the fuck out of here.'"

In the back of my mind, I knew that Towndrow was minimizing his involvement in the homicide. I let him continue because at least we were getting somewhere. We would figure out his complete involvement soon enough. For now though, I was interested in finding out where exactly they had left Daniel's body. The motive for the crime was becoming clear as well. Daniel had obviously been purchasing stolen military equipment from these guys and heat was coming down on them, so they killed him to keep him quiet. It almost sounded like the plot for a movie.

Towndrow continued to describe that Jones and Moore told him they killed Daniel by hitting him over the head and strangling him with 550 parachute chord. They had attempted to clean the scene with Windex. A few days after they dumped his body, the three of them returned. They believed Towndrow's truck would get stuck in the snow, so they drove Jones's truck which was equipped with 4-wheel drive. Out of concern that someone was going to find the body at the first dump site, they moved Daniel to a wooded area near the Tanana River south of Peger Road. Towndrow helped me draw a map to where the body was located.

At the conclusion of my interview with Towndrow, I called Chris and Dave and told them to meet me at the station. I also told them not to forget their snow boots. We grabbed a camera and some flashlights and set out to find Daniel Frederick.

We drove south on Peger Road and turned left on top of the dyke that runs east and west on the south side of town near the banks of the Tanana River. After a quarter mile or so, we turned right down a spur road that dead ended at the banks of a slough which flows into the Tanana. It was cold, about -20° F. The trail was just where Towndrow described it would be. It meandered about 50 yards into the woods from the end of the spur road. At the end of the trail was a partially buried, green military sleeping bag.

After taking some photos, I slowly unzipped the sleeping bag, exposing the battered face of Daniel Fredrick. He still had his hair, so I guess that answered the wig question. He was frozen solid. There were distinct marks on his neck where a ligature had been used to strangle him to death. We zipped the bag up and called the on-call funeral home. Daniel's frozen body, sleeping bag and all would be flown to the State of Alaska Medical Examiner's Office in Anchorage for autopsy.

I felt sorry for him. What a horrible way to die. They had beat him, strangled him, and thrown his body out in the woods. Daniel was no match for the men who had killed him. I doubt he put up much of a fight.

****

The day after we pulled Daniel Fredrick's body from its frozen tomb, Detective Chris Nolan and I went to the Fairbanks Correctional Center to re-interview Michael Moore and Raymond Jones. We interviewed them at the same time but separately. The interviews did not last long. Once both men were informed that Towndrow had talked and that we had found Daniel's body, they caved like a house of cards that was stacked too high. However, their version of events was a little different than Towndrow's, more specifically, Towndrow's involvement in the murder.

Jones told me that the three of them went to Blondie's the night of the homicide to steal back a lot of stolen military equipment they had recently sold. He continued to say that he waited in Towndrow's truck while Moore and Towndrow went inside the business. At some point they came out, and he helped them load the sleeping bag in the back of the truck along with other stolen items. Jones denied that he went inside the business until after the sleeping bag was in the back of the truck. Towndrow was attempting to clean up blood on the floor using a bottle of Windex. The two men told Jones that Blondie had tried to stab them with a screwdriver and they had done something "bad." They discarded the sleeping bag near the Tanana flats but returned a couple days later in his truck to move the body because his truck had 4-wheel drive.

Moore basically threw himself under the bus and took full responsibility for his actions. He told Chris the three men went to Blondie's that night because they thought they were being investigated by Army CID. They were afraid Blondie would rat on them to CID investigators so he and Jones contacted Towndrow to elicit his help in killing him. He continued to say that Jones waited in the truck while he and Towndrow attacked Daniel in the basement of the business, striking him to the ground before Towndrow strangled him with the 550 parachute cord. Moore even stated that his hand got caught under the parachute cord when it was wrapped around Daniel's neck so Towndrow had to let off the pressure so he could remove it. It was a great confession.

Over the next couple of days, we served several search warrants. In the bed of Towndrow's truck, we found trace amounts of blood that through DNA testing were later matched to Daniel Fredrick. The storage unit that Jones had rented on the Richardson Highway was also searched. Thousands of dollars in stolen military equipment were stashed inside. Backpacks, plastic totes full of helmet head lamps and assault rifle magazines were just some of the things we found. There was also a colonial era United States Flag stuffed in a duffle bag which had been on display in Blondie's

Antiques. We found drops of blood on the floor in the store's basement, even blood spatter on the limbs of a Christmas tree that was for sale. There was also an empty bottle of Windex.

We also served a second search warrant at the apartment on Kent Court. During Moore's interview, he stated that inside the residence was a suitcase full of stolen merchandise from the store. We had missed it during our initial search. Sure enough, in a closet by the front door was a black suitcase. Inside were all of the vintage baseball cards I drooled over as a kid. The same cards. Sitting on top of the cards was Daniel Fredrick's wallet. It's funny how things work out, right? As a kid I would sit and chat with Daniel about these baseball cards in his little shop on the corner. Years later, I was arresting three men for his murder.

During the process of writing this memoir, I promised myself I would try hard NOT to throw anyone under the bus, even when it comes to how this case was handled by the District Attorney's Office. I'm not a lawyer, and I don't pretend to understand all of the nuances and legal issues that are in play when a case is taken to trial. I do know, however, that there are certain legal issues which are considered when multiple defendants are taken to trial at the same time. Generally speaking, the statement of one defendant cannot be used against a co-defendant. For example, I can testify as to what Jones told me he himself did, but not what he said Moore or Towndrow did because Jones cannot be compelled to testify and has the right to defend himself against false statement. Moore's or Towndrow's attorney cannot cross examine Jones because no one can make Jones testify. I know it doesn't make a lot of sense to me either. It's called a Bruton issue.

In most cases where there are three defendants, the DA will plead one guy out in exchange for his testimony against the other two defendants. The Daniel Fredrick homicide case was, for all intents and purposes, a slam dunk. All three defendants had confessed to some degree. Even Towndrow, whose deal was off the table because he minimized his involvement, had essentially confessed. We had the body and an autopsy report confirmed that Daniel had been beaten and strangled. There was evidence that not only did they kill Daniel, they burglarized his business and then used his stolen credit cards to go on a shopping spree. All three of the defendants could have been tried on their own. The case was that good. There were no loose ends.

A couple of months before the cases were scheduled for trial, the defendants' lawyers started talking about plea deals. I called the district attorney who was handling this case and specially asked them for my superiors and me to be involved in any plea negotiations. This was a high profile case that had drawn quite a bit of media attention and it was a GOOD case. There was no reason for these cases to be plead out to nothing. I was told, "No problem." I understand that the police do not have to sign off on plea deals, but we are supposed to work as a team on murder cases. As detectives, we have a lot of time, energy, and emotions invested in each of our cases.

The very next morning, there was an article in the paper about the first of the three defendants pleading to a lesser charge. The very...next...day. I was livid. A couple days later the other two defendants also plead out. No one at the police department was ever notified that plea deals were in the works despite being told we would be consulted. I was flat-out lied to. I am the first one to tell a prosecutor if I feel a case needs to be plead or if a case has weak points that will not stand up in trial.

Not this case. I can only guess why this case was let go so easily, but to sit here and write about my speculations will only piss me off...more than I already am...still am after six years.

Raymond Jones was sentenced to twenty years flat time. He will lose a third of that twenty years for good behavior. Michael Moore got forty years but with twenty years suspended. He will serve twenty years but again, he will lose a third of those twenty for good time and then be on probation for ten years. Both men are eligible for discretionary parole after they serve a third of their twenty years. Brian Towndrow, because of his record and involvement in the murder, received seventy years with thirty suspended. But again with good time and discretionary parole, he will serve a fraction of the forty years. These three men planned and executed a calculated and premeditated murder. Criminals in Fairbanks who have been convicted in drive-by shootings where NO ONE was hit got more time than any of these murderers.

The police did their job. We did our job. Our team worked together and solved this case before Christmas.

The system failed Daniel Fredrick.

CHAPTER 8
DRINKS AND COFFEE CAKES

Kaylynn Bishop was weary after working another long shift waiting tables at the Hide Out Sports Bar & Grill. Another evening dealing with the rather eclectic crowd that frequented the Hide Out before it closed for business in the fall of 2012. It was after 4 A.M. before she was able to punch out on the time clock and although she was supposed to be at her third job by noon, Kaylynn had made plans to meet a male co-worker after closing to chat. The co-worker, like many of her friends, had become concerned because Kaylynn had been uncharacteristically depressed lately.

There was a slight chill in the early morning air as she made her way to the employee parking lot behind the building. A faint blue tint highlighted the eastern sky as the sun began its slow ascent above the horizon. It was May 6, 2012, and the days were getting longer. By the middle of June, the sun would barely dip below the horizon during the middle of the night. The long spring days are welcomed by Alaskans, particularly residents of the Interior, after having endured another seemingly endless dark, cold winter.

She drove to the Holiday Gas Station located at the intersection of Cushman Street and 23rd Avenue. While she waited for her friend to arrive, she purchased two coffee cakes, another snack cake and a drink totaling $3.41. She paid the clerk with four $1 bills. The clerk handed her a receipt and Kaylynn walked out the east entrance. The time stamp on the receipt showed 4:32 A.M. The transaction was recorded by high-definition surveillance cameras. Her French braids were clearly visible on the security footage as she walked out the door. Instead of tossing the receipt in the trash near the gas pump, she put the receipt in a storage compartment in the dashboard of her car, and she drove away.

Kaylynn drove just down the road to the parking lot of another business on the Old Richardson Highway. It was a convenient place to stop and chat with a friend for her, as it was on the way home. She still lived in a house owned by her family, passed down to her and her ex-husband, off Hartzog Loop in North Pole.

Her co-worker met her, they chatted, and about an hour later, they said goodbye, and Kaylynn continued her journey south on the Richardson Highway before she turned north on Badger Road. The final few miles along the Badger Road loop were peaceful, the calm before the storm she knew was coming. Her phone had been blowing up since closing time at the bar. Kaylynn turned onto Hartzog Loop before making a left on Toivo Court. Her house was at the end of the short road, situated on the bank of a small one-acre pond. She was met at the door by her live-in boyfriend, a man named Nyrobbie Chandler.

All she wanted to do was get some sleep. She had to be at work at the gas station around the corner in less than six hours. Chandler, who had been anxiously awaiting her arrival, had worked himself into a jealous rage by the time Kaylynn pulled into the driveway. He had called the Hide Out and her cell phone repeatedly with no answer. She barely got a foot in the door before Chandler started yelling, accusing her of being late because she was seeing another man. She was scared. Kaylynn had become accustomed to the screaming, but ever since she had threatened to leave Chandler, something had changed in him, something about the way he glared at her while he yelled.

He followed her down the hallway to the bedroom where he continued his tirade while Kaylynn changed out of her work clothes.

****

"Hey, you need to come to work," Kristi told me.

"What's going on?" I replied.

"A couple guys found a body, well at least they can see what looks like a foot sticking out of the ground. Lt. Soden is on scene by those ponds, just off the Rich near Badger Road."

"Okay, I need to swing by the station, and I'll head that way." It had taken a while, but I had grown accustomed to receiving calls from my wife telling me I needed to come to work, especially during the summer months when she worked grave shift in the City of Fairbanks Emergency Communications Center. Getting called out at all hours of the night is a part of the job you learn to deal with when you accept a promotion to detective. It goes with the territory. Regardless, the long nights and overtime shifts take their toll on family. I'm lucky because I am married to a woman who works in law enforcement, so to a degree she understands the stresses of the job. In all actuality, she works a lot more overtime than I do.

It was May 9, 2012 at about 9:00 P.M. when I received the call from dispatch. Luckily, I had just put our young twins down for bed so they wouldn't miss daddy that evening. The older kids were brushing their teeth getting ready to turn in because it was a school night. I gave them both a hug, and they wished me luck catching the bad guy, just as they had been doing since they were old enough to understand what their dad did for a living.

Badger Road is a major artery that runs in a loop around the Richardson Highway between the cities of Fairbanks and North Pole. As I drove toward the scene that evening, I was trying my best to get into crime scene mode. The Fairbanks Police Department does not have a crime scene unit. Our detectives work their own crime scenes, often with little or no help from outside resources. My mind was racing through a mental checklist of what needed to be done when I arrived. If it was human remains that had been discovered, I knew I was in for a long night and several days away from home.

Turning north on Badger Road, I made an immediate left on the Old Richardson Highway. I knew I was in the right area when I spotted two marked Fairbanks Police Department cruisers down the road. Stretching only about three quarters of a mile, this section of the Old Richardson Highway was rarely traveled. It had been abandoned and literally cut off by a man-made drainage ditch during construction of the *new* Richardson Highway. As I drove toward the flashing lights of the cruisers, I tried hard to remember the last time I had been down this road. Drawing a blank, I realized perhaps I never had been. There are a couple small ponds in the area that I suppose hold some fish, however locals know the area as a meeting place where men who advertise their "services" on various websites meet other men.

Lt. Soden met me as I climbed out of my car.

"Hey Matt, what do we have?" I asked.

"Well, we aren't real sure yet," he responded. "We were waiting on you guys to get here so we haven't done anything. Two guys were walking down this dirt road back to the pond to go fishing. They were looking at that old car down there, and they claimed to have found a foot sticking out of the ground. No one has been down there yet."

Lt. Matt Soden had nearly twenty years of experience with the Fairbanks Police Department by this time. I first met Matt during the summer between my junior and senior years of high school. I was bagging groceries at a supermarket located around the corner from my house. The store manager and I got into a scuffle with a shoplifter, and Matt was one of the patrol officers who responded. It was a comfort knowing he was the patrol supervisor on this scene. With his years of experience, I knew he wouldn't let anyone near the body or disturb any potential evidence.

A few minutes later, our investigations lieutenant, Lt. Dan Welborn, arrived on scene followed by Detective Chris Nolan. Lt. Welborn had been our supervisor for a little over a year after spending his entire career in patrol. His laid-back supervisory approach was well liked and appreciated by our investigations team. While he was the boss, he understood that the detectives in our unit knew what they were doing, so he did his best to let us do our thing and not micromanage our cases.

Prior to our arrival, there had been a conversation amongst the first responders about which agency should be responsible for the investigation in the event a body was discovered. An Alaska State Trooper unit had been first on scene, but the trooper left after determining the scene should be handled by the Army Criminal Investigations Division (CID) on Fort Wainwright due to our proximity to the base. CID investigators were called to the scene, and they figured it should be an Fairbanks Police Department case, so our patrol officers were called. This kind of back-and-forth case juggling is common at car accidents when one side of the street is in the city and one side is out. But if there was a body buried out there in the woods, that should have been the priority from the start, not whose damn case it would be.

We walked about hundred yards down a gravel road that circled a stagnant pond to a spot where an old white car had been pushed off the side of the road backward down a steep embankment. Based on its weathered condition, the car had been there for a couple of years. The trooper had told Lt. Soden that the foot was sticking out from under some brush behind the car. We stood on the edge of the embankment and scanned the area below from the road. In the fading light, I strained my eyes searching for a human foot amongst the brush. After staring at the brush pile for a few minutes, I finally made out the shape of a white tennis shoe entangled in the limbs.

I walked back up the road and retrieved the camera from the backseat of my car. All of the patrol officers were excused from the scene with the exception of one marked unit that would remain to secure the scene while we worked. I took dozens of digital photos as I slowly worked my way to the junked car. Step-by-step, I picked my way down the embankment to the area at the rear of the vehicle. I tried my best to stay off the most accessible route down to the car, figuring that was the most likely area where the suspect would have walked. Crime scenes are like first impressions, you only get one good crack at it, so the last thing you want to do is screw it up by stepping on and destroying valuable evidence.

After I finished taking the initial photos, Lt. Welborn videotaped the scene re-tracing my steps from the top of the road to the location of the body. Once completed, Detective Nolan slowly began removing the debris covering the remains. Limb by limb it was removed until a pair of legs stuck out from under a piece of material that appeared to have come from the trunk of the car. That too was removed, exposing the lifeless body of a middle-aged Caucasian woman.

She was wearing pants and a brown shirt, and her right sleeve was pulled down over her right hand. On her left foot was a white tennis shoe, but her right foot was covered only by a white sock. Her pants were buttoned, zipped, and secured around her waist in a normal position. Most of the time you can tell when a person's pants have been put back on them after death because they are never pulled up correctly and are often left unbuttoned. Her face was battered, covered with bloody abrasions, but there were no obvious signs of death. No obvious knife wounds or bullet holes or deformities in her skull caused by a blow to the head with a hard object. Her hair was pulled back in a French braid.

Her eyes were closed, but her body was in a relatively good condition because the level of decomposition was minimal. I surmised this was because her body was covered in a low shaded spot and the temperatures were still hovering around freezing at night. I remember thinking, standing over this woman I had never met, that perhaps she was somewhere watching us making sure we were doing our job correctly. It was our job to speak for her, to uncover the truth about how and why her life came to an abrupt and violent end.

Unable to find any identification in her pockets, I fought my discouragement. Although her fingerprints would be collected and examined during her autopsy, we would not receive those results for at least three days. The chances of clearing an arrest in a homicide case are significantly increased when a suspect is identified early on in the investigation. There was a high likelihood this woman knew her assailant, so identifying her was our top priority after conducting a thorough scene investigation. I contacted the on-call investigator with the State of Alaska Medical Examiner's Office in Anchorage and received permission to remove the body from the scene.

In the fading light, we searched the immediate area around the car for any items of evidentiary value. The search continued up the embankment and onto the road. We found a piece of duct tape and a few other items, but we had no idea if they were related to the scene. We collected them just in case we found out later the items were important. The decision was made to return to the scene in the morning to conduct a more thorough search in better light. A patrol officer was posted to secure the scene until daylight and the body was taken away by a funeral home. She would be flown to Anchorage the next day for autopsy.

I made it home in time to take a short nap and shower before I headed back to the office. Sleep did not come easily though. The vision of her lifeless body, thrown away like a sack of trash in the woods, occupied my thoughts as I tossed and turned. Her face was the first thought on my mind when my eyes opened. There were knots in my stomach fueled by bursts of adrenaline as I made the short drive from my home to the station. Who was this woman? Did she have a family? Was anyone looking for her? Neither Fairbanks Police Department nor the Alaska State Troopers had received any new missing person reports. Right now I felt helpless, and I feared the unknown, because I knew the clock was ticking. We needed a name, and fast.

****

At 8:00 A.M. the next morning, Thursday the 10th of May, Lt. Welborn, Detective Nolan, Detective Scott Adams, and I returned to the scene to continue our search in the daylight for any additional evidence. We scoured the area around the vehicle and the roadway before spreading out and walking completely around the pond and through the woods. The only item we found was a condom still in the wrapper labeled "HUGE." To this day, whenever Detective Nolan meets a new officer or someone from another department, he reaches into his wallet to present them a business card. When he opens his wallet, he lets the "HUGE" condom wrapper fall out. His response is always the same, "I'm sorry, it's just so huge!" It is a hilarious ice breaker for anyone with a sick sense of humor.

I forwarded photos of the woman's face to all the local surrounding law enforcement agencies, but no one had taken any new missing person's reports. Based on the condition of her body, I believed she had only been dumped in the woods at best a few days before she was discovered, so we were able to screen out any cold missing person investigations. Someone out there had to be looking for this woman.

After putting the kids to bed that night, I drove to the Starbucks at Barnes & Noble Booksellers to buy my wife a coffee. Due to our opposite work schedules, these late night coffee runs are often our only chance to see each other during the week. While I was in line, she called and told me there was a man named Mark Miller[25] in the lobby requesting to speak with an officer. He wanted to report his daughter as a missing person. I told her I was on my way, and she politely reminded me that since I was already in line I might as well get her a coffee. I had a sinking feeling in my gut that it was going to be a long night so I got myself one too.

I had never met Mark before, so I had no basis on which to form an opinion about his demeanor or how he carried himself day-to-day, but the man who stood before me looked scared. I don't know another way to describe it. He was dressed in blue jeans and an old camouflage military jacket. His long, brown hair was not brushed particularly well. When he spoke, I sensed pain in his

---

25 This name has been changed.

gravelly voice that only a worried father can detect. We had crafted a press release detailing the discovery of an unidentified body, but we did not disclose any details as to where the body was found. I decided not to mention the discovery to Mark, but rather listen to his story first so I could learn about his missing daughter. Perhaps he would describe a large tattoo or something else his daughter had that would eliminate her from being our Jane Doe.

Mark told me he had last seen his thirty-one-year-old daughter, Kaylynn Bishop, on Saturday the 5th of May. Kaylynn was living with her boyfriend, an African American male known to Mark as "D," at Mark's former residence off Toivo Court in North Pole. As far as he knew, Kaylynn had been dating D for about six months. He also stated that Kaylynn was in the process of moving to a new apartment because the Toivo Court house was going into foreclosure. Mark described Kaylynn as a divorcee whose ex-husband and three small children were living in Missouri. Kaylynn was trying to earn enough money working three jobs so she could afford to move to Missouri to be with her children.

Mark had seen Kaylynn on two occasions on the 5th of May. Kaylynn had borrowed his truck to take a load of trash to the dump from the Toivo Court house. When she returned the truck, her boyfriend, D, was following her in Kaylynn's black Saturn Ion. Kaylynn spoke to her father briefly before leaving with D. Later that day, Kaylynn stopped by her father's home on her way to work at the Hide Out where she waited tables. They chatted for a while, and Kaylynn asked Mark's girlfriend if she would put her hair in a French braid. When Mark made that statement my heart sank. I knew I was about to tell this man his daughter was dead. As she backed her vehicle down the driveway, Mark waved goodbye. It was the last time he would see his daughter alive.

In addition to her job at the Hide Out, Kaylynn had also been working nights at the College Road Taco Bell. She was supposed to begin work at her third job at Badger Gas, a small convenience store located around the corner from the house on Toivo Court, at noon on Sunday the 6th of May. Although the message was no longer stored on his phone, Mark recalled receiving a text message from Kaylynn at about 2:30 P.M. on Sunday the 6th of May. The substance of the text was for Mark to contact D to arrange a time on Tuesday for him to drop off Kaylynn's car at Lowe's Home Improvement where Mark worked. Mark did as instructed and called D, and the arraignments were made as requested.

On Monday the 7th, Mark stopped by Badger Gas to get a cup of coffee on his way to work. The employee working that morning informed him that Kaylynn had failed to show up for work on Sunday. On Tuesday morning, Mark again stopped at Badger Gas for coffee and was told that Kaylynn did not show up for work on Monday either. Concerned, Mark called Kaylynn, but after several rings the call went to voicemail. After hanging up, he immediately received a text message from Kaylynn's phone. The messages read as follows:

Kaylynn: "You called"

Mark: "Yes, u ok?"

Kaylynn: "Yes"

Mark: "Call me"

Mark: "Where are you"

Finally, on the 10th of May, Mark drove to the house on Toivo Court and saw Kaylynn's car parked in the driveway. Both of Kaylynn's dogs were outside running around in the fenced yard, and there was a note pinned to the garage door. The note read as follows: *"Harry I came by Lowe's a couple times and didn't see ur brown truck. I been done moving my stuff I forgot how to get to ur house been their twice. U call me 799-####. Key is in the car."*

During our conversation, Mark's girlfriend arrived at the police department and provided the same details about Kaylynn's last visit to their home to another officer. She also mentioned that Kaylynn had said something about wanting to go to Chena Hot Springs (a resort about fifty-six miles from Fairbanks). I had dispatch run Kaylynn's name through our internal report writing system. Kaylynn had been contacted by officers at a party in the downtown area in 2011. Also contacted at the party was a man named Nyrobbie Chandler. Running Chandler through the system revealed that he was an African American man who also went by the moniker, "D."

Unfortunately, no matter how many you do, death notifications are never easy. I will always remember my first one. I was dispatched to a residence to inform a mother that her daughter and son-in-law had been killed in a car accident in British Columbia while en route to Fairbanks. Their car had been crushed by a logging truck that had flipped over while passing them going the opposite direction.

In this particular case, I gave Mark a choice. I told him that we had discovered a body that, in my opinion, was more than likely his daughter. I could either show him a picture of her face to identify her, or we could wait a day or two for fingerprint identification. The choice was his.

I suppose Mark made the same choice that I would make as a father. He couldn't wait any longer.

I picked out a sanitized photo from the hundreds taken at the scene and placed it in front of him. He looked at the photo for a minute before looking me in the eye and saying, "That's Kaylynn."

We spoke a few minutes longer before Mark and his girlfriend left. Working death cases, you become used to the sadness and depression associated with the work, but as a father I couldn't help but break down inside. I thought about my little girl at home, cuddled up in bed next to her favorite stuffed animal, and having seen Kaylynn's body as it was, I felt a small sense of the pain that man must be going through. I promised Mark I would do everything I could to find out what happened to his daughter.

After they left, I returned to my desk and began scrolling through the hundreds of photos I had taken at the scene. Had we missed anything? It's easy to second guess your work and wonder if you missed a key piece of evidence. You just have to remind yourself that what is done is done and there is no turning back.

I printed off Kaylynn's DMV photo and compared the face pictured on her driver's license to the lifeless face I photographed at the scene. The two faces looked similar yet different. They shared some of the same facial features like the same shape around the eyes and nose, but at the same time they seemed like the faces of two different people. I pinned Kaylynn's DMV photo above my desk and placed another copy in the leather notebook I carry at work. I knew looking at her picture would give me inspiration when I would become frustrated during the investigation, as I was bound to do.

I started making a to-do list of investigative tasks that I would go over with our team as soon as possible. Now that we had a name to go with our victim, the investigation would kick into overdrive. It was close to midnight, so I was surprised when my desk line rang.

"Detective Merideth, can I help you?"

"Hi, my name is Sean Wilson, and I'm a manager at Taco Bell. I heard you guys found a body and well, one of my employees hasn't shown up for work, and I'm a little worried about her. Here name is Kaylynn."

I sat back in my chair and sighed. I knew I was about to pull another all-nighter. "Well, Sean, I would like to speak with you about that. Where are you now?"

"Well, sir, I'm at home right now, but I'm leaving in the morning. I have some weird text messages from her you may want to see."

He certainly had my attention. "What is your address, and I will be right there."

I was familiar with Sean's neighborhood not far from the police station, as I grew up in the same neighborhood and my parents still live just a few blocks away. Sean explained that he had not actually spoken with Kaylynn recently because he had been out of town. However, he had received several text messages from her on Sunday the 6th of May. Eventually I would obtain Kaylynn's phone records, but for now I photographed the messages on Sean's phone, which read as follows:

Kaylynn: is sean back

Kaylynn: cant get good phone service im in chena hot springs can some one cover me please

Sean: Ya I just got my pone just like 5 mins ago. Why can't you work tonight

Kaylynn: went to chena hot springs with some one that I met last night be back tomorrow

Kaylynn was supposed to be starting her new job at Badger Gas on the Sunday the 6th at noon. What was she doing at Chena Hot Springs Resort? That didn't make sense. Sean provided me with the names of two additional Taco Bell employees he knew had received similar text messages from Kaylynn over the past few days. Their names were Jose Gutierrez and John Gundersen.

At some point, the 10th turned into the 11th as I finished my interview with Sean. I called the number for Jose that Sean provided and was able to speak to him for a few minutes. We agreed to meet in a half hour at Walmart where Jose worked a second job.

My mind ran in circles during the short drive to Walmart. Who was she with at Chena Hot Springs? How did her body end up buried off Badger Road? Things weren't adding up; something wasn't right.

Like Sean, Jose had become concerned because he had not seen or heard from Kaylynn in the past few days—with the exception of exchanging a few text messages. Jose told me he had tried to call Kaylynn on the 7th between 8:30 and 9:00 P.M., but the call went straight to voicemail.

He also received a text message back right away that read, "Who is this." Jose described he texted back that it was "Jose" and asked if she would cover a shift for him at Taco Bell. The response from Kaylynn was:

Kaylynn: Im still out here

Jose: Where

Kaylynn: Chena hot springs@with a friend needed to get away

Jose: Are you working tonight?

Kaylynn: Be back Thursday

Jose told me he knew that Kaylynn had been trying to get a new job at Badger Gas and that she was still waiting tables at the Hide Out. What he told me next would set the tone for the rest of the investigation and would become a common theme during many of the interviews I would conduct with various co-workers and friends in the days to come.

Jose described how Kaylynn had been trying to break up with her boyfriend D for some time. She had confided in Jose that D was very jealous, but she'd found that breaking things off with her boyfriend was difficult because they lived together. Jose also shared how Kaylynn told him she was scared of D and that he had been getting into fights at the Hide Out while she was working.

The conversation I had with John Gunderson at Taco Bell was very similar. Although he had deleted the text messages, he had also been texting with Kaylynn about her missing work because she was at Chena Hot Springs with some guy she had met at the bar.

Clearly, we had to attack this investigation on two fronts. Did Kaylynn really go to Chena Hot Springs? And if so, with whom, and how did she end up buried off Badger Road some 56 miles away? Second, we had to start working the boyfriend angle.

These were the thoughts occupying my mind as I drove home in the early morning hours. The streets were empty, and I made every light. I pulled into my driveway and was silent as I slowly closed the door behind me trying not to wake the kids. I had to be in the office in five hours ready to brief our unit.

Once again, sleep did not come easy.

****

On May 11, 2014, an autopsy was performed on the body of a female preliminarily identified as Kaylynn Bishop. The autopsy was executed by the Chief Medical Examiner of the State Alaska, Dr. Katherine Raven, at the medical examiner's office in Anchorage. The autopsy was witnessed and documented by an investigator from the Alaska State Troopers.

At the conclusion of the autopsy, Dr. Raven ruled the manner of the death as homicide caused by asphyxiation due to strangulation. A set of fingerprints and a DNA sample from the victim were collected. Within days, the fingerprints were submitted to the Alaska Automated Fingerprint Identification System. They matched the fingerprints on file for Kaylynn Bishop.

****

I had just fallen into a deep sleep when the alarm clock rang on the morning of the 11th of May. I lay in bed for a few minutes thinking about the things I had to do when I made it to the office. I needed to brief the unit on the events of the prior evening and get to work writing several search warrants. Thoughts of Kaylynn ran through my mind, and they were the motivation that forced me out of bed and into the shower.

We round tabled around the coffee maker that morning at the department and prioritized what tasks needed to be completed. Detective Nolan and Investigator Gibson volunteered to drive to Chena Hot Springs to search for any evidence, either through surveillance video or credit card receipts, that Kaylynn had actually visited the hot springs alone or with a companion. I got to work writing four search warrants.

The first two search warrants covered the house on Toivo Court and Kaylynn's Saturn Ion for any evidence related to her death. To our knowledge, the Saturn was still parked in the driveway at the Toivo Court house. If we discovered that Kaylynn never went to Chena Hot Springs, I guessed she was killed in the house and her body was later dumped where she was discovered. It was just a hunch, but it would make sense with her body found just a few miles from her home.

The third warrant authorized the seizure of Kaylynn and Nyrobbie Chandler's cellular telephone records, including what cell towers any calls or texts pinged the day before Kaylynn disappeared and throughout the preceding week.

Finally, the fourth warrant authorized the electronic recording of conversations between Mark Miller and Nyrobbie Chandler. If we discovered that Kaylynn never went to Chena Hot Springs, Chandler was the most likely suspect in her murder. They were living together, and according to a couple of her co-workers, they didn't exactly have a great relationship. As I worked on the warrant, I called Mark and discussed whether he'd be willing to speak to Chandler about Kaylynn's disappearance. To our knowledge, no one else knew that Kaylynn's body had been discovered, even the employees from Taco Bell. I wanted to record Chandler's reaction when Mark told Chandler about Kaylynn's death. I was hoping he would slip up and we could catch him in a lie, or that he would say something we could use when the time came for a formal interview.

Just before lunch, I met with the Assistant District Attorney who had been assigned the case. She had prosecuted several serious felony cases I had previously investigated, including homicides. Her assignment to prosecute Kaylynn's killer was excellent news. We spoke about the circumstances surrounding the discovery of the body, and she reviewed the search warrants I had crafted that morning. After some minor tweaking, we walked to the court house and went on the record in front of a judge who signed off on the warrants with little fanfare.

At about 2:00 P.M. Mark arrived at the Fairbanks Police Department to call Chandler. Before we let him do so, Detective Nolan and I coached him on what he should or should not say. Detective Nolan had just returned from Chena Hot Springs without much information. Although it would be a couple days before we would receive the video surveillance footage, Kaylynn's name was not listed on the hotel registry, and her credit card had not been used at the resort.

After ignoring calls for twenty minutes, Chandler finally answered Mark's call. The two spoke for a few minutes about a trailer Mark had been trying to sell. I had encouraged the small talk, thinking that it would relax Chandler so that when the topic of Kaylynn was brought up, he would feel comfortable speaking to Mark about her.

"I'm just concerned because I haven't heard from Kaylynn, have you?" Mark finally asked after a few minutes.

Chandler replied, "No, I mean, I can forward the text message, I read the text message that she sent me, cuz what happened, I don't know what happened, if you look in the car there is a receipt, that was the receipt that she had, that was in there when she came back that night."

I heard the nervousness in his voice as he rambled through his answer. A simple "No" would have answered Mark's question, but Chandler wouldn't stop talking. He didn't know it, but he was painting himself into a corner and locking himself into a story. I made a mental note to check for a receipt in the car when we served the warrant later that afternoon.

Chandler went on. "Cuz you know, we were dating and then we talked one day when I picked her up from work and she was crying cuz she couldn't get her kids and was always somebody that was running bills, and she was like, she talked to me and she said she was going to move in with you and try and save the money and move to I think Missouri, and that is the reason we split up and everything."

Chandler and Mark then spoke about the events leading up to Kaylynn leaving for work Saturday evening, including the trip to drop Mark's truck off at his house. Chandler said, "She went to work, and I stayed at the house and went to sleep and then I woke around like four o'clock and called her, and she was like, 'I'm already leaving the store now,' and I was gonna ask her to bring me a soda. She came home, I was still sleeping, she came and her phone went off and we went to sleep, we woke up the next day, her alarm was going off, I was watching a movie and I was like your phone is ringing. She said, 'Oh, it's just my alarm,' and then her phone starting ringing and later on that time she got up and I was like, 'You need help doing anything?' I thought we were gonna do the yard and she was like, 'I have to go to the end of the mailboxes to meet somebody.'"

I assumed Chandler was referring to the row of mailboxes at the end of their road. He continued, "And then she came back, she came inside, and I don't know who, and then she grabbed all of her shampoo, she grabbed her jacket, she grabbed a clean shirt and a clean pair of pants, or some pants for work and she said, 'I'll see you after I get off work.'"

Chandler then said, "I didn't even know where she was going until she sent me the text message talking about, 'when I'm done using the car to call you (Mark) and everything and drop the key off. By the time I was done with the car I never seen your truck so I was—damn—I forgot how to get to his house.'" Chandler also said that he had tried to call Kaylynn several times, but that his calls kept going straight to voicemail.

Obviously, what Chandler spewed out to Mark during their conversation just didn't make any sense. In some ways, this was exactly what we were hoping for. He had somewhat locked himself into a story that we could use against him if we could prove Kaylynn never left the house alive. I found it hard to believe, even without having done much background on their relationship, that Chandler would just let Kaylynn leave the house, supposedly with another guy to go to Chena Hot Springs Resort. Not to mention that she had to work at noon at Badger Gas. The pieces of the puzzle were starting to come together, slowly.

At about 8:00 P.M., Detective Nolan, Lt. Welborn and I responded to the Toivo Court house to serve the two warrants I had obtained that morning. I also asked Sgt. Jeremy Rupe from the Alaska State Troopers Alaska Bureau of Investigation (ABI) unit to come with us. The Toivo Court house is outside the city of Fairbanks, and while FPD officers have statewide jurisdiction, I thought it was a good idea to have an ABI investigator involved in the investigation. I've known Jeremy for nearly my entire career, and I consider him one of my closest friends. One of his favorite pastimes is taking my money playing poker on a routine basis.

Squatting at the end of a cul-de-sac, the faded brown single-story house had certainly seen better days. My first impression was that the house and the lot it was built on had the potential of being very attractive because the lot sat on the banks of a small pond. Kaylynn's black Saturn Ion rested in the driveway, looking fairly clean. I guessed it had been run through a car wash before being parked there.

We had not been at the house five minutes before Mark pulled into the driveway to deliver the key that would let us into the house. He was on the phone, which I didn't think much of it until another car pulled up behind his truck. The driver was female, but the passenger was a bald, black male whom I immediately recognized from his DMV photo as Nyrobbie Chandler.

Chandler, also speaking on the phone, emerged from his vehicle. I quickly realized that Mark and Chandler were speaking to each other, and Mark was recording their conversation with a recorder we had given him. I immediately walked up to Mark and introduced myself, hoping he would get the hint and play along.

He played the part perfectly, asking questions about why we were at the house and who we were. Chandler never suspected Mark and I had met before. I explained to Mark that we were following up on a missing person report filed by some of Kaylynn's friends and that I would call him later. After Mark drove off, I reached into my shirt pocket and activated my digital audio recorder and approached Chandler.

"Hey, how you doin'?" That was best I could come up with at the moment. "I'm with the police department."

"Is everything okay?" Chandler asked.

"My name is Detective Merideth, and this is Detective Nolan, and we are with the Fairbanks Police Department. Do you live here?"

Chandler was stuttering as he responded, "I was staying with Kaylynn, we were together, and have been dating since Thanksgiving."

"Oh, so you don't live here anymore?" I asked.

"Well, no, she sent me a text, she left Sunday, she sent me text that she was going to Chena Hot Springs. She wanted me to get all my stuff and said I could use her car and told me to get all my stuff out." Chandler was so nervous; he was shaking and his voice was quivering when he spoke. He added that the house was being foreclosed and that Kaylynn had put $400 down on another apartment on Chena Pump Road.

"She came in (from work) and said that she was going to go meet somebody at the mailboxes because they didn't know how to get here. She came back and grabbed her stuff."

Pulling out his phone, Chandler showed me the text messages that he claimed Kaylynn had sent him. I didn't want to spook him by photographing the messages on his phone, so I read them aloud in order to record on my device. Though the messages might be forensically recovered from his phone at a later time, even if they were deleted, I wasn't going to count on that. It was a good thing I didn't.

I read off Chandler's phone, "'From Kaylynn...I am going to Chena Hot Springs so when you are done moving your stuff can you please take my car keys to my dad's work ask for Mark Miller, he will be there on...'" The message ended. The text was sent on May the 6th at 3:45 P.M. Chandler also explained that sometimes Kaylynn carried two phones, one being a pre-paid cell and the other a regular subscription cell through a local phone company. This information would become very important once I received the phone records for both Chandler and Kaylynn.

Chandler pointed out that he had used Kaylynn's car to run up to Badger Gas to get her a mocha when she returned home from work late at about 6 A.M. Sunday morning. He also described the receipt he had discovered in the car which listed two drinks and two coffee cakes.

This was now the second time Chandler mentioned finding the receipt. Finding it was obviously important to Chandler. Were drinks and coffee cakes his motive for killing her? Did he think she had bought food and a drink for another guy? Or was he using the receipt as an alibi, and whoever she was with at the Holiday station must be who she had run away with.

Chandler took back his phone and showed me a missed call from Kaylynn later in the evening on the 6th. He kept talking. He told me he had dropped off Kaylynn's car at the house just a couple days ago when he was through moving.

When he finally quit rambling, he gave me his phone number, and I told him we would stay in touch. I never mentioned the discovery of Kaylynn's body. His story would be easy enough to prove or disprove through Kaylynn's phone records.

After Chandler left, we entered the house which was empty with the exception of an old couch in the living room. In an attempt to be thorough, an officer opened the foul-smelling refrigerator, making the search less pleasant. The carpets were neglected and full of stains, and the walls were covered with a mystery liquid. It reminded me of dozens of houses I had been in over the years that left me wondering, "How do people live like this?"

There were no obvious signs of a struggle or big puddles of dried blood on the floor. We sprayed some BLUESTAR around, a substance that glows in the dark when it comes into contact with blood, but nothing really jumped out at us. In the end, we seized a large section of the living room carpet, and we swabbed a few areas on the walls just in case the substance that fluoresced was blood.

We impounded Kaylynn's car and towed it to Fairbanks Police Department. The car was probably the best place to find any items of evidentiary value. After all, Chandler had told me that he had been using her car since he had last seen her, even up until just a couple days ago. Perhaps her body was transported in her own car to the dump site in the woods? We were going to find out...and luck would be on our side.

****

I would like to think that over the years I have learned to be a compassionate and good listener. Someone victims and their families can trust and confide in. That was proving to be difficult in this case. Kaylynn's mother, Karrie, lived in Idaho. Normally communicating with family members living outside Alaska is not a big deal. However, this case wasn't normal.

During the infancy of this investigation, we were doing our best to keep the fact that Kaylynn's body had been a found a secret. This allowed us to work covertly gathering evidence and conducting interviews while people, certainly the suspect, were not aware the police were one step ahead. While I had not done anything wrong, I still did not feel right about not having spoken with Kaylynn's mom. Mark Miller had become a major participant in the investigation, and he was her nearest next of kin. I had relied on him to speak to Karrie on my behalf.

After several days, the Fairbanks Police Department put out a press release detailing the discovery and identification of Kaylynn Bishop. It was after that, while I was at home eating dinner with my family that I received a call from Karrie. I stepped out onto our deck for some privacy, not wanting Karrie to hear my kids chatting and laughing in the background.

I tried to comfort Karrie, but what do you say to a mother who has just lost her child? She asked for reassurance that I was doing my best to find out what happened to her daughter. She wanted details about how Kaylynn had died and where her body was found. Did she die instantly? Did she suffer? Was she raped? I told her as much as I could without compromising the investigation. Perhaps I told her more than I should have, but I had to tell her something.

One of the worst parts of policing is explaining to grieving parents about how their children died. But it's a part of the job I've had to learn to accept.

Once we decided to release the identity of the Jane Doe, the press hounded us seeking more information. I was actually very impressed that we had been able to keep things as quiet as we had for more than a few days. Once the press started calling and asking questions, it became apparent they had no idea about the exact location she was found or any of the circumstances regarding the investigation. This worked to our advantage.

The day after we gave the press release, I was contacted by a woman named Patricia Potts. Ms. Potts came to FPD believing she had some information pertinent to the investigation. She told me she owned an apartment building in the University West section of town just outside the Fairbanks city limits. She continued to explain that a couple weeks ago, she was approached by Kaylynn Bishop about renting an apartment. Kaylynn had gone to her office with a guy she assumed was her boyfriend. Ms. Potts accepted a $400 cash deposit and Kaylynn filled out the rental application.

She didn't think much about it until a few days ago when she began getting some strange text messages from Kaylynn. When she found out Kaylynn was dead, she came directly to the police. The messages read as follows:

Kaylynn: "hello are u at work by chance"

Ms. Potts: "No. Who's this?"

Kaylynn: "Kaylynn that but the money down on apt is their any way I can get that to day im leaveig state"

Ms. Potts: "Call me"

The following day the messages continued.

Kaylynn: "sorry I didn't call after work I got the flu im gonna send a friend to pick up the half the money please let me get at half back I can really use it now"

Kaylynn: "if u cant do it please let me no thank u"

Our investigative team had all but ruled out the possibility that Kaylynn had traveled to Chena Hot Springs. There was no evidence to suggest she had, however with the discovery of these text messages, my mind was made up.

Kaylynn never went to Chena Hot Springs, and she sure as hell never sent these messages to her future landlady. By this point,

I had interviewed at least five of her friends who all told me she was trying to get out of her relationship with Chandler. They had described Chandler as being very jealous and Kaylynn was afraid of him. The first step was finding a new place to live, and she had done that. My nine-year-old son could type a text message and spell better than this. After learning about Kaylynn, I was certain she could as well.

In the forensic bay at the Fairbanks Police Department, Kathi Young examined Kaylynn's Saturn Ion. Kathi is a crime scene technician with the State of Alaska Crime Detection Laboratory, and the only technician assigned to Fairbanks. Kathi worked all day, patiently scouring every inch of the car. By this point in the investigation, I was fairly certain that Kaylynn had been killed in her home and transported to the dump site in her own car.

One of the first things Kathi discovered was a receipt from the Holiday Gas Station on 23rd Avenue tucked away in the center console. The receipt showed that a hot beverage and two coffee cakes were purchased at 4:32 A.M. on May 6th. That would have been just after Kaylynn would have gotten off work at the Hide Out.

There was no obvious blood in or around the car's trunk, only a red liquid that seemed to have been poured on the bare floor. The car's carpet had been removed. Kathi sprayed BLUESTAR on the rubber seal around the trunk's opening. Several areas on the rubber seal glowed, so Kathi took samples. A presumptive test for blood was positive.

At about the same time Kathi was working her magic on the car, I received pages of cellular telephone records from the legal department at GCI (General Communication Inc.). Fortunately, the cell phone records had been downloaded into a spreadsheet that was fairly easy to decipher. Incoming and outgoing calls and text messages were listed in separate columns and the same for text messages. There was also a separate listing for the cellular tower the call or text pinged off when it was initiated. The legal representative from GCI was nice enough to provide me a listing of the location of each cell tower.

I spent some time going over the records trying to assign a name to the phone numbers listed on the records. There were two important things to consider when reviewing Kaylynn's phone records. I had spoken with several people, like Ms. Potts and her

Taco Bell co-workers, who told me they had received text messages throughout the week from Kaylynn. Some of them even said Kaylynn was already at Chena Hot Springs and had invited them to come on out. I had to confirm that those text messages were sent from Kaylynn's phone and what cell towers the texts were pinging off.

All of the text messages sent from Kaylynn's phone after the 6th of May pinged off cell towers in the Fairbanks or North Pole area. Many of them pinged off a cell tower located just around the corner from her home on Badger Road. A horrific picture was forming in my mind of the truth of Kaylynn's final moments.

I have always been a believer that the simplest explanation as to how or why a crime was committed is usually the right one. It is very easy to over complicate things and come up with conspiracy theories about this or that. It might be good fodder for a one-hour television show, but that is not the real world. By the time I finished going through her cell phone records, I was convinced that Kaylynn had been the victim of a domestic violence-related homicide committed by an extremely jealous boyfriend and fueled by her coming home late from work.

What if she had just thrown the receipt away?

I couldn't help but think that a little piece of paper was the difference between her living and dying.

Two coffee cakes. One word: two.

He had found the receipt, probably after relentlessly questioning her about where she had been and who she had been with. Chandler's phone records showed he called the Hide Out several times and was blowing up Kaylynn's phone after closing. I can only imagine his jealous state of mind, how he had worked himself up by the time she made it home.

The time had to come to confront Chandler and to close this case.

The time had come for a little justice for Kaylynn.

****

By the 15th of May we had the case pretty well figured out— or at least we hoped we had. I had interviewed scores of Kaylynn's friends who essentially all told me the same thing: Kaylynn was involved in an emotionally draining relationship with a jealous boyfriend that she was desperately trying to get out of.

Chandler had even been issued a trespass warning from the Hide Out and was not allowed inside because he was continuously harassing Kaylynn's male customers. He was known to follow her around at work to make sure she did not spend too much time at any particular table. All of the interviews painted a very grim and disturbing picture.

Since identifying Kaylynn's body, I had been in touch with the District Attorney's Office every day to keep the prosecutor up to speed on any new developments. I enjoy working with the attorneys assigned to my cases, and since our unit primarily deals with violent crime, we end up working with the same violent crime attorneys all the time.

At this point, we had built up enough probable cause to arrest Chandler. Obviously, we needed to conduct a thorough interview with him about the case, and we would on several occasions. However, the evidentiary case against Chandler was stacking up.

Every prosecutor wants a smoking gun, the eye witnesses who say they saw the whole thing or the suspect's fingerprint in blood at the crime scene. In this case, it came down to identifying the contributor of the blood found in the trunk of Kaylynn's car. Juries love to hear about DNA evidence. We call it the "CSI Effect." Most jurors watch television and all of the detectives staring in true crime television shows solve all their cases in forty-five minutes based on DNA results that come back from the lab in five minutes. The average citizen has no idea how long it takes to get DNA results back from the laboratory. A rush job on DNA can take between three to six weeks depending on any number of variables.

Unfortunately for us, there was one huge variable during the summer of 2012. The State of Alaska Crime Detection Laboratory moved. I don't mean they moved some equipment around the office or moved their gear down the hall; they moved to another building.

On television they would like you to think that you can just unplug the "DNA machine" and plug it back in and away you go. It doesn't work that way in real life. Not only that, this is the government we are talking about. It's not like when you move to a new house and you pick a day and rent the U-Haul truck, have some friends over for pizza and move some boxes. The government doesn't work nearly that fast.

I was told the DNA results on this case could be expected by the middle of August...and it was only the middle of May. The D.A. made it very clear that she wanted the DNA results from the blood in the trunk before we made an arrest or took the case before the grand jury. I tried hard to understand her position, but at the same time it was very frustrating.

On May 15th, I received a telephone call from Chandler. I was a bit surprised when he called, but it wasn't a big deal, and it wasn't unusual for suspects to contact me during an investigation. I had conducted a dozen interviews with potential witnesses to Kaylynn's last days, and the case had progressed to the point where we were ready to interview him. When he called, he asked who he was talking to and I explained I was the detective he spoke with at Kaylynn's house a few days ago.

He said, "I don't know what's going on, but people are talking about how I did this. After I talked to you gentlemen, I had a weird phone call, and I recorded half of it" He pulled out his phone and found the date and time of the call. Then he pulled up a blocked number. "And a guy called my phone and the guy said 'let me talk to Kaylynn right now.'" There was a tremble in Chandler's voice.

"He started asking me questions about 'did I hear about them finding a pair of legs on the Badger overpass?' And he was telling me that she was cut up and everything like that and they found a head here, they found a torso here..."

I told Chandler that I had already spoken to the person who called his phone; I wasn't bluffing, I was that far ahead of him. "Would you be willing to speak with me so we can sit down and talk about the case?" I asked him.

His first choice for a place to meet was McDonalds.

Yeah right. I don't think so. I wanted to speak to him in a more controlled environment than in the kid's play area sharing some McNuggets. "You know, it would be easier if you just came to the station in a couple hours," I said casually.

He agreed.

Chandler arrived at the station at about 1:30 P.M. Detective Nolan and I brought him upstairs to the investigation division, and he had a seat in our main interview room, which is wired for high definition sound and video.

It was very important to me that Chandler felt comfortable despite the cramped room. At least comfortable enough to want to talk to me but still know that he was in *my* world.

I had already made the decision that this interview would be what we refer to as "non-custodial," meaning that Chandler would be told he was free to leave at any time and that he was not being detained. By doing so we avoided the requirement of reading him his Miranda Warning, which advised him of his rights to remain silent and have an attorney.

During the interview, Chandler made several admissions regarding some topics that never came up during our brief initial contact with him. He mentioned the receipt he had found in the car, but this time he admitted that he had been "sneaky" and that he went snooping around in her car after she got home from work. He told a long story about how he had been asleep when she got home from work and that some time that morning she got a call from some guy he did not know. Kaylynn mentioned something about having to meet someone at the mailboxes at the top of the road. She took off in her car but returned a few minutes later, gathered up some clothes and left with whoever she had met.

We tried our best not to push Chandler too hard during this initial interview. If he didn't confess to the murder right away, we wanted to preserve the chance to interview him again. If he lawyered up, then we would lose our shot. Of course, what Chandler was saying did not make any sense. He wanted us to believe that he just sat in the house while the woman he loved and lived with took off with some guy to who knows where and he didn't mind? Add to the mix his explosive and jealous personality we'd heard about, and I did not believe a word he was saying.

There were two important questions we asked Chandler during the interview that, depending on the answer he gave, would really paint him into a corner and lock him into a fabricated story.

Kaylynn had two cell phones she used on a regular basis. One was a "track phone" or pre-paid phone for which we could not access phone records. The other was her standard GCI cell phone, and I had already spent hours analyzing those records.

I asked Chandler on which phone Kaylynn had received the call from the guy who picked her up at the house. His answer?

Her GCI phone. But according to her phone records, Kaylynn never received a call at that time.

We also asked Chandler if anyone else beside him had been using Kaylynn's car the past week. If DNA tests revealed the blood Kathi found in the trunk was Kaylynn's, it was important to know if anyone else had been in possession of her car. His answer? No one but him had been using her car.

There was no way to verify Chandler's story about what happened that morning after Kaylynn got home late from work. Perhaps that's why he thought it sounded so good. Based on her phone records though, we could disprove that she ever received a call from a mystery man who picked her up at the house.

As we promised at the conclusion of the interview, Chandler walked out of the Fairbanks Police Department just as he had walked in: a free man. That was painful to watch, but I knew he wasn't going anywhere, and if he did we would find him. There was still work that needed to be done, interviews with Kaylynn's friends and co-workers I had yet to track down. But I had time. The DNA testing was going to take months, and as it turned out, it was a very, very busy summer for our unit.

****

As May turned to June, business picked up for the department as it tends to do during the summer months in Interior Alaska. We kept tabs on Chandler and interviewed everyone involved in the case no matter their involvement.

It's a strange thing to say, because it was a homicide case, but we kind of ran out of things to do while we waited patiently for the DNA results. Cases tend to come in peaks and valleys. You can go for a couple months with only a few good cases trickling in here and there. Those times are good for catching up on paperwork. Then *wham!* You get nailed with several big cases at once, and you don't see your kids for a week.

On the 27th of June, two transients called 9-1-1 from a pay phone at Walmart and reported a woman was being beaten at a homeless camp on the north side of the Johansson Expressway near Walmart. Patrol officers responded quickly to the scene and discovered a woman named Ellen Rada lying on the ground unconscious. They also found a man named Rick Allen. The camp was in a wooded area and it appeared Ellen and Rick had been living there off and on in a tent. A small campfire was still burning. The officers called for paramedics, who responded and attempted unsuccessfully to wake Rada. There were no obvious injuries on her face or body, so everyone assumed she had passed out from drinking. She was transported to the Fairbanks Memorial Hospital (FMH).

Her visit to FMH didn't last long. A head scan revealed her skull was badly fractured and her brain was beginning to swell. She was medevaced to the Alaska Native Medical Center (ANMC) in Anchorage where she remained in a coma for several days until she passed away without regaining consciousness. While Ellen was fighting for her life, I was playing politics and dealing with red tape bullshit with ANMC. I had to have multiple medical releases signed by Ellen's family to get anyone, even just a nurse, to give me an update on her condition. Finally, I just had an investigator from the Alaska State Troopers go to ANMC and speak to the staff directly. I knew her skull had been cracked since the staff at Fairbanks Memorial Hospital had told me that. But before I went looking for the assailant, I needed an update.

Dealing with crap like this is very frustrating when you are trying to stay on top of a violent assault case that will likely turn into a homicide investigation. After she died, but prior to her autopsy, I got on the phone with a lady from human resources at ANMC. She informed me that, although we had a medical release on file for Ellen, we needed yet another release signed for a doctor to speak with me about her death.

Furious, I called my lieutenant over to my desk because I wanted him to hear exactly what I was about to tell this lady. Before I even spoke, I knew she was going to file a complaint against me, and she did, so I figured why make the boss play catch up?

I laid into this lady with everything I had about how her nonsense privacy restrictions that NO other hospitals have in Alaska do not apply to law enforcement in emergency situations. The clock was ticking, and every second I spent dealing with this crap was time I was not out looking for and interviewing the man who killed Ellen.

Maybe I just cared too much, but I was pissed, and I let her know it.

My boss was laughing the whole time. It was great.

When I hung up on her, his phone rang five minutes later... and then *he* gave her an earful!

Five minutes after that Detective Scott Adams and I both received calls at the same time from two different doctors explaining exactly what injuries caused Ellen's death. The information was important because before we interviewed Rick, we needed an idea of which side of her skull had cracked, the size of the fracture, how hard of a blow would be needed to cause the fracture, etc.

Immediately after speaking with the doctors, Scott and I left the station and drove to a homeless shelter of sorts in south Fairbanks. We found Rick eating dinner alone. Having encountered Rick as a patrol officer years ago, I recognized him right away. The first thing I noticed was that he was eating grilled red salmon over rice. Really? They serve grilled red salmon at this place? Dang.

For the better part of an hour, we talked to Rick about what happened between him and Ellen the night she was taken to the hospital. It took a while, but eventually Rick admitted he had sucker punched Ellen really hard on the side of her head and knocked her unconscious. He was upset because he thought she had been cheating on him, and he was drunk at the time. We left Rick at the shelter that evening with the promise we would return the next day and perhaps take him to the scene so he could reenact exactly what had happened. I wanted to arrest him, but since we had conducted a non-custodial interview, meaning that he was free to leave when we finished, we couldn't detain him right away.

The next day, Scott and I picked up Rick and drove him to the homeless camp. I was videoing while Scott and Rick walked through the scene. Rick showed us in detail how and where he assaulted her. When he was finished, Scott looked at me and asked, "Can you think of anything else?" Just then I realized I had never hit record! Yikes! I played it off as best I could.

"Uh, Scott...I think we should have Rick run through it one more time just to make sure we get all the details. You know, sometimes it takes a couple times to remember everything...uh... right?"

And that is exactly what Rick did without missing a beat. I thanked my lucky stars he didn't lawyer up before doing that second reenactment. I didn't tell Scott what I had done until we got back to the car.

Looking back, it's pretty funny, but not so much at the time! Months later Rick Allen pleaded to a manslaughter charge in the death of Ellen Rada and was sentenced to eight years in prison. I did not agree with the length of the sentence, but then again, I'm not a lawyer.

Three weeks later we were hit again. On the east side of Fairbanks near Fort Wainwright there is a neighborhood called Birchwood Homes. The houses were originally built for the military in the early '80s but have since been converted to civilian housing. My father actually did the plumbing on many of the houses when they were under construction one summer when he was not teaching.

On the 17th of July, a woman came home from work to an eerie silence. Her young teenage son should have been home. She called out, but no one answered. She walked upstairs and discovered a gruesome scene. A young black male, about the same age as her teenage son, was lying dead in their spare bedroom. There was a lot of blood on the floor and a gun was near the body. She called 9-1-1 to report that she had found a dead kid in her house and her son was missing.

Lt. Welborn[26] and I responded to the house in the Birchwood neighborhood and began our investigation. The streets were filled with kids and nosy adults gawking at the house, all of them wondering what the commotion was about. After speaking to the woman and her husband, a soldier who had just returned home from Afghanistan, we pieced together what happened. The young black male was a friend of their son who was still missing. The gun on the floor next to the body belonged to the missing kid's father and was usually kept in a nightstand. The parents' bedroom door was usually locked. Not this day.

An hour later the woman's son returned home crying and upset. He got scared when he shot his friend by accident, so he ran away from home. He made it an hour. I interviewed the kid in his living room with his parents present. I was as compassionate as I could be. One young man was dead and this kid, nearly the same age as my oldest son, was going to have to live the rest of his life reliving the moment he shot his best friend in the head. He saw the blood, he saw the body hit the floor and felt the recoil of the pistol in his hand. For such a young boy, I can't think of a worse punishment than that.

---

26 Dan Welborn retired in 2020 as Deputy Chief after 25 years of service with FPD.

That evening, I spoke to the mother of the kid who was shot and killed. Parents are not supposed to outlive their children. It is very painful to make these notifications, especially to tell a mother of her young son's life cut short. In this instance, the mother did not want the young boy who shot her son charged with a crime. It was an accident. Two kids playing with a gun they had no business looking at, let alone touching. I agreed with her. Should the parents of the shooter be charged? I don't know. That decision was left up to the lawyers, and they were not charged. I am not sure if the military disciplined the father.

For me personally, it was another young child who died before ever having a chance to live. Like so many times before, I hugged my own kids extra tight that night when I returned home well after their bedtime. I didn't even care if I woke them. Hearing the loving, "Hi, Daddy," was music to my ears. I tucked them in and walked across the hall into our bedroom and put my Glock in the safe on the floor next to my side of the bed. I made sure it was locked.

Lightning struck again four days later on Glacier Avenue in the Hamilton Acres neighborhood, not far from Birchwood Homes. Built in the oil rich pipeline days of the late '70s, Hamilton Acres is the neighborhood where I grew up. My parents still live there in a house we moved into when I was in fourth grade. As far as crime goes, it's always been a fairly quiet residential area, but in recent years as the neighborhood gets older, crime has picked up considerably. A woman called 9-1-1 after hearing gunshots fired in the apartment next door. A second 9-1-1 caller, this time a neighbor a house away, reported seeing a young male carrying a handgun running into the woods behind the complex.

Patrol officers arrived and found that two males had been shot inside the apartment. One guy was shot through his right arm. The second was shot through the abdomen and lying on the living room floor going in and out of consciousness. He was scooped up by Fairbanks Fire Department paramedics and rushed to FMH. His prognosis was not good.

Other patrol officers entered the woods behind the apartment complex looking for the man who'd fled. They found the guy, identified as Christian Williams, hiding in the woods near a slough just upstream from the Chena River.

The case seemed simple enough. Lt. Welborn and I were called out and responded to FMH to interview the victims. Patrol had secured the scene pending a search warrant, and they were also looking for the gun presumably dropped by Williams in the woods. We tried to talk to the guy who had been shot in the arm, but that didn't get us anywhere. He was not exactly a fan of law enforcement, so we got the familiar, "I don't know who shot me," or words to that effect. The gut-shot victim had been rushed into emergency surgery. He was shot through the pancreas and was not expected to survive.

After speaking with some family and friends at the hospital, we went to the station and sat down with Williams, who had previously waived his Miranda Warning. Williams told us, and I'm not making this up, that the two guys he had shot had made him play Russian roulette, so he shot them. He also told us the gun was an automatic, which made sense because we found spent casings at the scene. I'm not exactly sure how you play Russian roulette with an automatic, but that is what he said happened, and he would not budge off his story.

We took him back to the scene to show us where he threw the gun, but we couldn't find it. As we were tromping around the woods, a call came in for patrol officers to respond to a possible self-inflicted gunshot wound across town. A few minutes after they arrived on scene, the officers requested a detective respond. Since I was knee-deep in the current case, Detective Adams volunteered to go. I spent a couple more hours looking for the gun in the woods. We never found it, and to this day it has still not been recovered. I have a hunch that Williams threw it in the slough.

We spent the rest of the night processing the scene inside the apartment. We could tell by the location of the shell casings that Williams was sitting where he said he had been, or at least in that general area. I was still having a hard time buying the Russian roulette story. The gut shot victim made it through surgery, but he was being flown to a special trauma unit in Seattle. I made it home at about 2 A.M. and crashed in bed. My phone rang three hours later.

Sgt. Kurt Lockwood, a close friend of mine for fifteen years, was the first officer on scene for a reported domestic assault, also in Birchwood Homes. The caller, the young wife of a soldier just home from a deployment and had been arguing with her husband about an affair she had been having. She would later describe that she and her husband, Robert Evans, returned to their residence from a night of drinking at a nightclub with a friend of hers. Evans was sleeping on the couch, and she and her girlfriend were chatting in an upstairs bedroom. Evans snuck upstairs and eavesdropped on the conversation in the bedroom through the door. Evans and his wife both stated during their subsequent interviews that Evans believed his wife was texting a guy she had been having an affair with.

Evans kicked the door open. He pulled a gun on her, and she ran outside and called 9-1-1. Evans ran after her and struck her in the face. He told his wife, "There will be bloodshed if the cops show up." Evans went back into the house. When Kurt pulled up to the residence, Evans immediately took fire from an upstairs bedroom. One bullet struck Kurt's patrol vehicle. He slammed his SUV cruiser in reverse while more shots were fired.

Officers from every department in the area responded to the scene. Evans emerged from the residence. He still had the pistol in his hand. It seemed like for an instant that Evans was going to take the easy way out for him and force one of the officers to shoot him. Our guys showed a tremendous amount of restraint and talked him into dropping the gun. He was taken into custody without further incident. That is something you don't hear anything about in the media. If Evans had been shot it, it would have been national news. I can see the headline: "Soldier Shot After Returning Home From Deployment." Instead Evans was alive because our officers acted with a tremendous amount of professionalism and restraint and talked that gun out of his hands. You won't see that in a headline.

I drove to the station where I interviewed Evans and his wife. Evans had been drinking but he was sobering up. During the interview he admitted that he had pulled the gun in the bedroom and that he had struck his wife. He basically confirmed everything his wife had already reported. Additionally, he told me he thought the vehicle he was shooting at belonged to the guy his wife had an affair with coming to pick her up. As Kurt was driving a fully marked Fairbanks Police Department SUV with a light bar on top, I knew that was a lie. But Evans never admitted he was shooting at a police officer even though he told his wife there would be bloodshed if the police came. Evans was arrested that morning for attempted murder and several other firearms related charges.

Lt. Welborn and I drove to the Evans residence and met Detective Alana Malloy[27] from property crimes and Investigator Gibson who were both processing the scene. Kurt was still there, and I'm not ashamed to say I gave him a big bear hug, thrilled to find my friend still alive. Nine spent .40 caliber shell casings were discovered inside the residence on the upstairs landing where Evans had positioned himself. Three rounds that hit the roof outside the window were directly in line with Kurt's patrol vehicle. The fourth shot hit the front bumper.

The scene was being taken care of, so it was time for breakfast. Lt. Welborn and I drove to The Bakery Restaurant and sat down for a nice meal. I was starving, but my eyes felt like sandpaper. Then the phone rang. It was dispatch.

"Hey, Peyton, did you respond to that suicide last night?"

"No, I was busy working the scene on Glacier. Scott went but patrol handled the report. Why?"

"Well, CID is bringing two soldiers to the station. They say they were there when it happened, and it was a homicide."

The first words that came out of my mouth were, "Oh, shit."

At this point, about all we could do was laugh at the situation we found ourselves in. We finished our breakfast in a hurry and drove back to FPD. To say we were behind the power curve on this case was an understatement. The scene had been released back to the apartment owners and the body was gone. We were going to have to work backward depending on what these new witnesses said.

The shooting occurred at 1313 22nd Avenue apartment #11 which was a one-bedroom apartment on the second floor. The previous evening when patrol responded, they found only two people besides the deceased in the apartment. Their names were Josh and J. Gordova[28], the wife. The body of a young soldier named Michael Brooks[29] was found in the living room. He appeared to have died from a gunshot wound to the head. Near the body was a .45 caliber Springfield pistol wrapped in a green towel. The magazine had been removed. Two live .45 rounds were found, one in the living room near the body and one in the kitchen.

The stories the Gordovas gave to the officers seemed to match. They both stated that Michael was a friend of theirs and

---

27 Alana Malloy is currently a detective with FPD. We attended Lathrop High School together.

28 Both names have been changed.

29 This name has been changed.

that he and Josh had gone through basic training together. After a night of bowling, they returned to the apartment and continued drinking. At some point, Joshua got out his new pistol and they started playing with it after removing the magazine. Then Michael either accidentally shot himself in the side of the head or committed suicide. At some point, Josh and J. mentioned that he was sitting in a chair in the living room when the shot was fired. Both of the Gordovas, especially Josh, were visibly upset. Michael's body was collected by the on-call funeral home, and the scene was released back to the Gordovas.

The case appeared to be either a tragic accident or a suicide. Fast forward to the next morning when Lt. Welborn and I found ourselves interviewing two soldiers, M.G. and J.C., both of whom stated they were in the apartment when Michael was shot and that it wasn't a suicide. I spoke to J.C. while Lt. Welborn interviewed M.G.[30]

J.C. described that he and M.G. were picked up by the Gordovas who had been at the bowling alley on Fort Wainwright with Michael. The group went back to the Gordova's apartment to hang out. They did not stop anywhere along the way. J.C. told me that they had only been in the apartment for twenty minutes when Michael and Josh emerged from the bedroom and that Josh was carrying his pistol. Josh and Michael walked through the apartment and into the living room where Michael got down on his knees. J.C. said it looked like Josh tried to clear a jam in the pistol before he put the gun to the side of Michael's head and pulled the trigger.

At the shot, J.C. and M.G. ran out the back deck door and down the stairs. He heard the gun drop to the floor and M.G. shout, "What the fuck?" as they ran from the apartment. They eventually met up down the street and called another friend for a ride. A couple of hours later, J.C. called his mom and told her about the shooting. She called the military police.

M.G. gave a similar story to Lt. Welborn. He thought the shooting was probably an accident since Josh and Michael were such good friends. He believed Josh had tried to clear the weapon before pulling the trigger and that Michael had said, "Shoot me." Both Josh and Michael were very intoxicated. M.G. was surprised that Josh even got the gun out in his inebriated condition.

---

30 Both names have been changed.

Since neither Josh Gordova nor his wife knew the police had been contacted about the shooting, we decided the best course of action was to obtain a warrant allowing us to record conversations between Josh and one of the two soldiers. But which one? Well, J.C. called his mom after the shooting and M.G. called his girlfriend.

We chose to use M.G. who was more than willing to wear the wire and meet with Gordova and his wife. After I obtained the warrant, we dropped M.G. off at the residence and parked nearby. Through the sensitive microphone, we heard him walking up the steps and knocking on the door. A neighbor must have heard the knocking, because a woman stuck her head out her back door and told M.G. the Gordovas had not been back to the apartment since the police left. In a way that was good news for us. Perhaps they had not cleaned the scene.

It had been a long couple of days, so we decided to call it an evening and go home for dinner. I had just sat down to the first meal with my family in three days when the phone rang again. This time it was Gordova's captain. He had found out about the shooting and heard we were looking for Josh and his wife. It seems that one of our patrol officers had given Josh Gordova a ride to the Fairbanks Memorial Hospital the night of the shooting. He had voluntarily checked himself into the psychiatric ward. That piece of information had slipped through the cracks. Meanwhile, his wife had checked into a hotel on Fort Wainwright.

I finished dinner and called Lt. Welborn. We agreed to meet at the station and drive onto the military base together. She was checked into the Northern Lights Hotel. We got lucky and she was in her room when we arrived. I explained to her that we needed to speak to her about the shooting and that she was not being detained by us and that she did not have to speak to me if she did not wish to do so. She agreed to talk. Again, this was one of those non-custodial interviews where Miranda warnings were not required.

She began by telling us the same story she had told the patrol officers that both Josh and Michael were intoxicated and that she was sober, then that Michael had accidentally shot himself while playing with her husband's gun. It didn't take us long to convince her that she needed to be honest about what happened.

She stuck with her original story a couple more times until I told her that M.G. and J.C. came forward. That changed her tune.

Her husband and Michael had been in the bedroom together. Josh came out carrying his pistol. He tried to clear it, ejecting a live round in the process. Michael got down on his knees and said something about Josh shooting him in the head. Josh did exactly that and a put hole through his temple.

After the shooting, his wife picked up the gun using the green towel and racked the slide, ejecting another live round. She also took out the magazine. This would account for the two live rounds found on the floor in the apartment, one in the kitchen and one in the living room. I guess Josh, in his drunken state, thought he had cleared the pistol when he ejected the first round. In reality he just loaded another round in the chamber. It was becoming clear that we didn't really have a homicide case, more like a manslaughter or criminal negligent homicide. Josh and Michael were close friends that had gone through basic training together and were stationed together in Fairbanks. There was no animosity between them. They were being stupid and playing around with a loaded gun when they were drunk. Simple as that.

Lt. Welborn and I left the base and drove to FMH. Although I had responded to the psychiatric ward on the 4th floor as a patrol officer, I had never actually interviewed anyone up there. This was going to be a little different. We met with Josh in his room. Because Josh was not free to the leave 4th floor, although he could have told us to leave his room, I read him his Miranda Warning, which he verbally waived and agreed to speak to me.

Josh was a mess. He started out telling us that Michael had shot himself, but it only took about a minute of convincing him to tell us the truth for him to change his story. He would not come out and tell us that he had shot Michael, but he said he could feel the recoil in his hand when the gun when off. He was crying hard. He was not faking it. He had shot his best friend in the head and he had to live with it. Case Closed.

The wheels of justice turn slowly. Months went by before these cases were adjudicated in the legal system. I referred the shooting case of the young man in Birchwood Homes to the District Attorney's Office for prosecution. As suspected, they declined to prosecute the kid, which did not sit well with the juvenile authorities. But I agreed with the prosecutor's decision. Seeing his buddy drop to the floor is all the punishment that young man could handle—or needed. That case is a textbook example of why you must keep your guns locked up and away from your kids.

Over two years later, the shooting on Glacier Avenue is still not resolved, although I just received word the suspect is expected to change his plea to guilty on two counts of Assault in the First Degree. The lawyers are working out the details, so who knows how long that will take.

To everyone's surprise, the victim that was shot though the pancreas on Glacier Avenue survived. During the course of our investigation, we found out that he was also a suspect in a sexual abuse case when we ran his name. Of course, he was arrested when he returned to Fairbanks from Seattle for Sexual Abuse of a Minor in the Second Degree. He was sentenced to six years with three years suspended.

Robert Hansen[31] was arrested and charged with Attempted Murder and various other assault and gun related charges. As required by law, his case was brought before the Grand Jury within ten days of his arrest. His wife testified that because of his military training and experience, if he really wanted to have killed Officer Lockwood, he would have. The grand jury, in one of the most unbelievable judicial screw ups in modern times, failed to issue a true bill.

Hansen was not indicted for his crimes, despite the fact that he admitted to intentionally shooting at the vehicle regardless of who he believed was behind the wheel. Talk about a slap in the face to local law enforcement. For the grand jurors to believe there was not enough evidence to take this case to trial, which is all a Grand Jury indictment really is, is unconscionable. In my opinion, they broke their oath as jurors.

Thankfully, because he was in the military, we had another alternative to pursue. In my opinion, the case had nothing to do with his experience in combat (except taking the high ground offensive position) or PTSD as would be claimed later. A jealous husband thought his wife was texting the guy she had been sleeping with. He beat the crap out of her, wouldn't let her call 9-1-1 for help, and then shot at the cops when they pulled up. Simple as that. The JAG (Judge

---

31 This name has been changed.

Advocate General) office on base agreed. Hansen was immediately charged by the military with essentially the same crimes he had been charged with in state court. The charges in military court stuck, and he changed his plea a few months later. He is serving a few years in a military prison, although I am not sure for exactly how long.

The summer of 2012 was busy. Our unit was shorthanded, but we made due and closed some good cases. I have only highlighted some of the more serious assault and death cases and left out the sexual assault and sexual abuse cases that constantly pile up. Throughout the summer, Kaylynn Bishop was not far from my mind. I stayed in contact with the crime lab and the D.A. while waiting on the DNA results. And one day out of the blue, I got an email from the crime lab.

****

On August 16, 2012, I received an email with an attached lab report from the State of Alaska Crime Detection Laboratory. It had been over three months since Kaylynn's body was discovered buried beneath a pile of logs and sticks in a ditch off Badger Road. We pared down six swabs from the dozen collected to send to the lab for DNA analysis.

In a perfect world, certainly on television, all of the samples would have been tested. But in reality, the complexity of the DNA testing process and the backlog of cases awaiting analysis make testing more than a few samples per case impractical. Of the six samples we forwarded to the lab, one yielded a positive result. The sample was collected from a piece of carpet from the side of the trunk of Kaylynn's car. The lab report read:

63250KV (Sample 63250-A from the piece of carpet)

> *DNA from at least two individuals was observed in this sample. DNA from a male individual was observed in this sample. Kaylynn BISHOP cannot be excluded as the source of DNA detected in the major component of this sample. No conclusions are reported as to whether Nyrobbie CHANDLER contributed DNA to this sample.*

The origin of this sample was a small drop of blood. We were never able to determine, even after sending the sample to a private lab for further testing, if Chandler was the contributor of the DNA found in the remaining part of the blood sample. The DNA was too degraded to match enough genetic markers for a positive comparison to Chandler's DNA, although it was very close. Regardless, Kaylynn's blood was found in the trunk of the car.

The DNA results confirmed our theory that Kaylynn had been murdered in her home by Chandler. He put her in the trunk of her own car and drove her to the ponds where her body was discarded and buried. She had never made plans to go to Chena Hot Springs that morning. A mystery man did not pick her up and take her out of town as Chandler had suggested. She was killed in a jealous rage by an out-of-control boyfriend.

The district attorney gave us the green light to arrest Chandler, and I immediately put the word out to our patrol officers to start looking for him. Early the next morning, Chandler was spotted by Officer Dustin Stonecipher in a local club. He was detained and transported back to the Fairbanks Police Department. Detective Nolan and I received the call at about 1:00 A.M. that he was on his way to the station. We drove to FPD and sat down with Chandler one last time.

This time I read Chandler his Miranda Warning, which he verbally waived and agreed to speak with us. The interview lasted about 18 minutes. Even confronted with the mountain of evidence against him, Chandler did not waver from his story. You can't argue with people like Chandler that stick to the same idiotic story they know is not true no matter what evidence is put in front of them. They have told the same lie so many times to so many people that even they start to believe parts of it are true. They don't know what else to say. More often than not, most people confess when they are put in the position Chandler was in. He was just digging a deeper hole for himself. By seventeen minutes and twenty seconds into the interview, I'd had enough. I put the cuffs on Chandler myself and placed him under arrest for the murder of Kaylynn Bishop.

Murder cases take forever to make their way through the court system. There are status hearings, calendar calls, and often evidentiary hearings well before a case is set for trial. In the months following his arrest, Chandler was examined by two psychiatrists in Anchorage. His attorney requested the interviews, I guess to determine Chandler's state of mind at the time he murdered Kaylynn while taking into account mental and physical abuse he had suffered as a child.

The interviews backfired. During both interviews, he admitted to killing Kaylynn in the bedroom of the residence after she got home from work that morning. They had gotten into a fight about her getting home late and possibly seeing another guy. Both psychiatrists found, in general terms that I can understand, that Chandler was fit to stand trial.

Not long after the interviews in Anchorage, Chandler plead guilty to Murder in the Second Degree. On November 5, 2013 he was sentenced to ninety–nine years in prison with thirty-four years of those suspended.

I agreed with the charge. I don't believe Chandler planned to murder Kaylynn when she returned home that morning. I think he lost control of his emotions during a confrontation with her in the bedroom. He said he lost it when she threw a shoe at him, and she was found wearing only one shoe.

I still had questions, questions that may never be answered. What happened to her shoe? Where was her cell phone, the one Chandler used to text and impersonate her? Where was the carpet from the bottom of the trunk?

I know in the big picture that those trivial things don't really matter, but they were loose ends in the investigation that I wanted to tie up. More than likely, I will never get my answers.

As I had done so many times before, I sat in the courtroom during the sentencing listening to Kaylynn's family speak to the judge about what they believed a fair sentence should be. Kaylynn's mother had flown up from Idaho for the proceedings. The day before I'd met her at the District Attorney's Office. Karrie was seated when I walked in the room. She got up and gave me a huge hug and thanked me for arresting the man who killed her daughter. I was so proud of the job our team had done on the case. We worked together to solve a difficult case, a case that began with an unidentified body in the woods all the way to a conviction inside a courtroom.

****

Later that fall, I was awarded the Meritorious Service Medal for my work on the multitude of cases I was assigned over the summer. My supervisor, Lt. Welborn nominated me for the award, and for that I am grateful. The letter of commendation that was presented with the medal read as follows:

> "For outstanding investigative work on multiple homicide cases. All six cases involved single or multiple victims of gunshots or serious physical assaults resulting in death or serious physical injury. All were thoroughly investigated by the Investigations Divisions with the following results: Case #12-1636, Carl David Jr., was arrested for Murder I, Murder II and Assault III for the beating death of a two year old child; Case #12-2028, Nyrobbie Chandler was arrested for Murder I after beating his girlfriend to death and dumping her body; Case #12-2886, Rick Allen was arrested for Murder II after a woman was found beaten and unconscious in the woods and later died; Case #12-3249, a juvenile was charged with Criminally Negligent Homicide following the shooting death of his friend; Case #12-3295, Christian Williams was arrested for Assault I in the shooting of two other people at a party; and Case #12-3297, Joshua Gordova was arrested for Murder II for the shooting death of a fellow soldier at his home. Detective Merideth was assigned and has been the lead detective in all six of these cases. Six homicides in a little over six months is remarkable, and the results obtained have been the same. His exceptional investigative skills and tireless efforts reflect great credit on him and the Fairbanks Police Department."

In in all honesty, it was just the luck of the draw that I was assigned all of these serious cases in such a short amount of time. With Detective Nolan out of service after back surgery and other detectives on leave here and there, well, I was the only general crime detective left in the office. But, it is what it is, and looking back, I think it was the support of my family that meant more than anything.

All of those cases represent a lot of late nights and early mornings. A lot of days away from home. I hate not being able to tuck my kids in at night, and I missed an awful lot of those special moments that summer. But every time I got pissed because I wasn't at home with my kids, I thought about Kaylynn's parents who will never be able see their daughter until one day they are reunited in a much, much better place.

CHAPTER 9
THE HORRIBLE AND THE BIZARRE

A triple homicide-suicide at a local hotel had me calling in while I was off duty. The scene was a single hotel room that had been secured by patrol officers before detectives arrived. The gruesome scene shook these hardened patrol officers, some of them veterans of the force, to their core. I have no doubt what they saw still troubles them to this day. It's cases like this that the public doesn't hear about, doesn't want to know about, and quite frankly, probably doesn't care about because they don't have to deal with it.

Our investigation revealed that the adult son of the family was upset the rest of his family, including his long-time girlfriend and infant child, were moving out-of-state while he was not able to leave Alaska (I can't recall why). I am sure he had some underlying mental health issues, and we later learned that he was verbally and emotionally abusive toward his girlfriend. The family was using the hotel as a staging point before driving out of Alaska.

A family staying in the room across the hall heard what they thought was gunfire and called 9-1-1. When the first officers on scene arrived, they went through the door and had to push loaded luggage carts out of the way. Every single person in the room was dead. The mother was lying on top of the girlfriend in the corner of the room. The baby was strapped in her car seat on the bed, and the son was lying in the middle of the floor. When the scene was secured, paramedics came in the room and confirmed all inside were deceased.

Based on the position of the bodies, it made sense that the son shot and killed his girlfriend before shooting his mother, who had stepped in front of the girlfriend probably to protect her. With the two women dead, he turned and shot his infant daughter in the head with a 10 mm pistol. This beautiful little girl was defenseless, strapped into her car seat when he put a bullet in her head. He saved himself for last and shot himself in the head.

Our investigations unit worked the scene for several hours, documenting every detail, taking photographs, and making scale diagrams of the scene. When it came time to remove the bodies, the mother and the girlfriend were taken out first. I guess the funeral home worker was trying to save some time, because when he loaded up the shooter on the gurney, he put the baby—still strapped in her car seat—on top of her father's body. Every officer on the scene objected to the baby being carried out with her murderer. Absolutely not. That little girl was wrapped in a blanket and carried to a waiting vehicle by a police officer.

We later discovered the girlfriend had been secretly recording their fights. It was painful listening to the way the father of her child treated her and controlled her. This girl was literally recording all these fights just in case someone, somewhere down the road, needed proof that she was living with a monster. We were too late.

****

Some scenes are so bizarre that its hard to figure out what happened. I can't count the times I have stood in the corner of a room, usually the scene of a death, and muttered, "What in the hell happened here?" It's mind boggling, and I suppose fascinating, how some people die. Some die naturally, some are murdered, and some decide exactly how they want to check out and reside permanently below ground. And in Alaska that may take a while because the ground is so frozen, funeral homes store your body until spring when you can dig a hole in the ground.

Early one cold January morning, our investigations team was called out to a house in South Fairbanks where the naked body of a young lady had been found lying on the garage floor. The woman and her boyfriend had been staying in the home as payment for renovating the house. Next to her body was a broken toilet that appeared to have originally been sitting on a dolly. Hanging from the garage door frame, the part that runs down the middle where the chain attaches was a yellow electric extension cord.

Her boyfriend told us he woke from a deep sleep to find the victim was gone. He searched the house and found her in the garage, sitting on the toilet with the cord wrapped around her neck. He unwrapped the cord and pushed her off the toilet which caused it to fall off the dolly and break into several pieces.

Our team was trying to make heads or tails out of the scene, trying to prove or disprove the boyfriend's story, when Lt. Welborn made the comment, "I don't think that garage door frame could hold her weight."

"Well Lt....uh....it *does* hold the garage door up, right?"

"Oh yea, duh."

As it turns out, the woman had wheeled the toilet to the center of the garage and tied one end of the extension cord around the garage door frame and the other end around her neck. She sat on the toilet and rolled backwards to take out the slack and then just leaned forward to cinch the cord around her neck, cutting off blood flow to her brain.

****

The Northward Building in downtown Fairbanks was built between 1950 and 1952 and still stands as one of the tallest buildings in town. Made of up of mostly low-income apartments, it is known to law enforcement as a melting pot of varying socio-economic situations and where radios never work because of the metal siding on the outside of the building.

One summer afternoon, my lieutenant and I were called to the Northward Building to investigate the suspicious death of a young woman who lived alone. She was discovered by a co-worker who was concerned because our victim had not shown up for work, something out of the norm for her. The co-worker contacted management, who opened up the apartment door to let us in. Standing in the doorway, they saw the victim covered in blood, sitting on the floor, and leaning up against the couch with her head resting on her arm. If it were not for all the blood, you would think she was taking a nap.

My initial impression of the scene was that the girl had been the victim of a robbery and murdered. The contents of her purse were dumped into a pile on the living room floor. The only piece of clothing she had on was a white tank top. Large bloodstains had soaked into the carpet around her purse and her computer, which lay on the floor plugged in near the couch. There was blood spatter all over the walls. There were also a lot of empty beer cans on the kitchen counter and in the trash can.

The deadbolt was locked from the inside, and we found her house keys on the table. Generally, homicide victims are, well, dead, which makes it difficult to lock the door as their assailant is fleeing the scene. However, I have investigated at least one homicide, which coincidentally occurred in the Northward Building, where the victim was severely beaten but managed to lock his door as his assailant ran out of the apartment. The victim in that case bled out internally over the next three days before succumbing to his injuries.

My lieutenant and I stood in the corner of the room for at least an hour surveying the scene and kicking around ideas about what may have occurred. Based on the position of her body, we could not see any obvious injuries that would have been the source of so much blood. A small wooden crate being used as a coffee table was in front of the couch. On top of the crate was a bowl with what looked like tomato soup filled with broken glass. On the floor near her foot was a broken drinking glass.

After the scene was photographed, we pulled the girl off the couch and onto the floor. Lividity, the pooling of blood to the lowest soft tissue, was fixed and rigor mortis was leaving her body, so she had been dead at a minimum for over twelve hours. The lividity, evidenced by the purple bruising on her legs and arms, matched the position of her body on the couch. This meant that where she was found is where she died; her body had not been moved. The only visible mark on her body was what appeared to be a puncture wound on the underside of her left arm.

An autopsy would be the only way to tell for sure how the young lady died, but our best guess at the time was that she was probably intoxicated when she fell and landed on the glass. The glass broke and penetrated an artery in her left arm, which would account for all of the arterial blood splatter on the walls. If that scenario were true, then the rest of the clues fell into place. Usually, not always, the simplest explanation is correct.

After she cut her arm, she picked up the broken pieces of glass and put them into the bowl of soup. Then she began walking around the apartment looking for her cellular phone to call for help. She dumped out the contents of her purse on the floor and even checked near her computer where perhaps she had left the phone on the charger. After losing too much blood, she felt tired and decided to sit down, rest her arm against the couch and go to sleep. There was no blood found in the bathroom where her phone was sitting on the edge of the sink.

****

Not long before retiring, I responded to a horrible suicide at an apartment complex in west Fairbanks. A group of guys had been at the shooting range all day and retired to an apartment for a night of drinking, not the safest combination of activities. At some point, one of the guys became upset when he saw a post on social media about his ex-girlfriend hooking up with another guy. He picked up an AK-47, put it under his chin and pulled the trigger.

When officers entered the apartment, there were guns all over the place and bottles of all variety of beer and hard liquor everywhere. A couple of us ran to the guy who had shot himself, but part of his brain was hanging out and his eyes were fixed and starting to glaze over. I felt his neck for pulse. Suddenly, the "dead" guy let out a gasp of air. It scared the absolute shit out of me. I literally jumped. It was a like a scene from *The Walking Dead,* and this guy was passing over to the other side. It still gives me the chills.

****

Call outs do not stop, not even on Super Bowl Sunday when Peyton Manning is playing! I was pissed! February 4, 2007, I was sitting in church hoping the preacher would preach a short sermon so I could get home to pregame before the big game. I was born in Tennessee, so my parents raised me as a huge Manning fan and today was going be his day! But no, someone decided to whack someone, so I had to go to work. I met Chris Nolan down the street from the address on 22nd Avenue. It was only about -20° F, so things were manageable and not too miserable.

This case turned out to be one of those "you can't make this shit up cases." Remember that scene from the *Wizard of Oz* when the Wicked Witch of the West's feet were sticking out from under the house that landed on top of her? That was the first thought that popped into my head when I noticed two feet sticking out the rear end of a car parked in the driveway. Under the car was the frozen body of an elderly lady who had obviously been dragged quite some distance and left under the car for dead. None of the officers had attempted contact at the house, so Chris and I knocked on the door which was answered by the homeowner.

In our typical bull-shitting friendly manner, I said, "Hi, we are detectives with the Fairbanks Police Department, and we are looking for the owner of the car outside."

"He's asleep on the couch."

To set the scene here, the owner of the house was in a relationship with another guy who came home drunk last night with the unknown guy, who was now passed out on the homeowner's couch. If he was upset before, he was really pissed now that the police were knocking on his door. Still, he invited us into the house and Chris and I sat down and woke up the owner of the vehicle.

Although groggy, and obviously still intoxicated, we questioned him about where he had been driving last night, who else was with him, etc. We never told him why we were asking him all these questions. After a few minutes, we had established that he was the sole driver, that he and his companion had met at a bar across town, and most importantly, that he was drunk when he drove home—although he defended this because he was "more sober than the other guy."

Finally, and I will never forget this, in his most concerned voice, Chris said, "Well, the reason we are asking you these questions is because there is a dead body under your car."

From a back bedroom we hear, "I told you we hit some... thing!"

Yeah... I think I'll go talk to *that* guy.

Sure enough, these two clowns were trashed and decided whoever was least drunk between the two of them and therefore the most capable of driving should drive home. Somewhere on Gillam Way, about a half mile from the house, they hit something in the road and kept on driving.

We continued our questioning, locked the driver into his story and eventually arrested him on the scene for driving under the influence. The charges were eventually upgraded to manslaughter.

We turned the driver over to patrol for processing and began to work the scene. We called a tow truck and lifted the rear end of the vehicle off the ground. This poor old lady had been dragged face down for blocks. Her face was chewed up and her butt cheeks had been scorched by the catalytic converter or the exhaust. Either way, it was a horrible way to die. An autopsy would later reveal her death was caused by her chest being compressed between the car and ground.

As a side note, I made it home for the second half of the game and watched Peyton Manning win his first Super Bowl.

****

In January of 2014, I attended the two-week homicide investigation class at the Southern Police Institute on the University of Louisville, KY, campus. It was a good class and I learned a lot and made some lifelong friends. When I returned to Fairbanks, I didn't even make it to the office on my first day back to work before I was called to assist our unit at an apartment complex fire, not far from my house. The large complex was a total loss, burned to the ground. At least 100 people were displaced and many of them had been transported to the Fairbanks Memorial Hospital for burns, smoke inhalation or hypothermia. It was nearly -30° F.

Our first job was to make sure that everyone who lived in the two-story building was accounted for. That task proved difficult because all the tenants were spread out across town. Some were still on scene, some were at the hospital, while others had gone to stay with family or friends. It took hours but we finally narrowed down the number of missing tenants to two people, both females who lived alone and next to one another on the second floor.

Although we couldn't yet prove the fire was set intentionally, we had a pretty good idea that it was arson. Shortly before the 911 calls started coming in about the fire, a juvenile named Connor Groppell was transported to the Fairbanks Memorial Hospital by ambulance for burns to his hands and arms. He was met by paramedics at a business across the street from the burned down apartment building. The timing of the 911 calls reporting the fire, and the 911 call from a business owner reporting that Groppell had run into his business yelling for help, was no coincidence.

The owner of the apartment building told our team that she had recently installed security cameras on the first and second floors. The storage hard drive for the camera system was located in a room on the west end of the first floor. This of course presented a problem because the building had collapsed and had turned into a huge pile of smoldering burnt sludge that was starting to freeze. Still though, we spent the night looking for the hard drive in the area where the room *used* to be. It was tedious work and we were all tired and freezing. It took hours but we found the needle in the haystack. The hard drive was found under a pile of smoldering debris. It was dented, burnt, and covered with ice. I was afraid we would break the Secure Digital (SD) storage card if we tried removing it. My vote was to send it to the crime lab to let someone else break it, but Detective Malloy thought otherwise. She slowly removed the SD card, which appeared intact.

Despite our best efforts, we couldn't get the security footage stored on the SD card to play. The file system for the security camera would only play on *that* system which was a pile of burnt junk. We took the SD card to a local computer shop and explained the problem to the technicians. These guys were great. It took a couple of hours, but the technicians got the video to play using a program they downloaded from a Japanese pornography website. Yea, if we had only thought to try *that*.

We searched through the files on the SD card until we found, literally, the smoking *person*. Groppell could be seen on the video carrying a gas can into the apartment of one of our missing female residents. A few minutes later, a bright flash explodes from the doorway and out comes Groppell, running down the hallway on fire. Literally, he was on fire.

We were working off the theory that Groppell had killed the woman in the apartment and had started the fire to cover up his crime. The woman who lived next to the apartment where the fire started was still not accounted for, so we assumed she had died in the fire as well. Next came the task of searching the burned, frozen rubble for the bodies of the two women. We knew where in the building their apartments *should* have been but finding evidence of their apartments proved to be an arduous task in the freezing cold. We searched throughout the day and into the night. Finally, on the second day of searching, we found the charred head and torso of the woman who lived in the apartment where Groppell started the fire. Here arms and legs had burned in the fire, but her chest cavity and neck were intact. Her face was burned away. She looked like a burned mummy. It was horrible.

Later that day we found the remains of the woman who lived in the next door apartment. Her remains were like the first victim. Not much of her was left after she burned in the fire. We found her lying on the coiled metal springs of her mattress. It looked like she had died in her bed, sleeping peacefully.

We never figured out the relationship between Groppell and the woman he murdered. An autopsy revealed the first victim had been strangled to death. No smoke was found in her lungs so she was already dead when Groppell left the apartment and returned with the gas can he used to start the fire. The poor lady who lived next door was deaf. She never heard the explosion or the commotion in the hallway as people ran for their lives to escape the burning building. She was asleep and died of smoke inhalation. She never made it out of bed.[32]

---

32 Groppell was charged as an adult with two counts of murder and arson. In 2019, 5 years after the fire, he plead guilty and was sentenced to 85 years in prison.

CHAPTER 10
INNOCENT VICTIMS

Murdered children cases are the worst. I don't know if I feel this way because I have children or if it is because I have witnessed the horrible things evil people are capable of doing to children.

Children are defenseless and too often are the target of angry parents who are hell bent on hurting someone to make themselves feel better. Either way, some cases burn a hole in your brain and keep you up at night thinking about the horrors you've seen, touched, and even smelled.

A couple of years ago I was teaching a general death investigation class during a spring session of the police academy when a student in the back asked a common but rather frightening question. He was a big, young, muscular kid, obviously a type-A personality. We were discussing interviewing sexual abuse suspects.

"Detective Merideth, how do you sit across from guys that murder or rape kids without punching them in the face? I couldn't do that, because I would just want to kill them. I couldn't control myself."

I responded, "Well, perhaps you've picked the wrong profession then." I probably embarrassed him a bit, but that was not my intention. He asked a smart-ass question, and he thought everyone in the class was thinking the same thing he was, but they weren't.

I followed up my initial knee-jerk response with, "Listen, does the end justify the means? By that I mean, does getting mad and assaulting a suspect solve the original problem? That being that your suspect has killed or raped a young child? The answer is no, it only makes matters worse. Our job is to protect children and put the bad guys in jail. We do that by getting confessions, not by beating their head against a wall like on television."

This is particularly true when it comes to investigating cases where a child was harmed and interviewing the suspects in these cases. As the interviewer, you must get inside the suspect's head and figure out why they hurt the child. Was the child crying too much? Did the child pee in the bed? Was the twelve-year-old girl wearing pajamas that were too provocative? It may sound sick, but these are all themes that suspects use to justify hurting a child.

I believe that most people want to tell the truth. they want to explain why they committed their crime because they want to be understood. They want someone to listen to their reasoning and be empathetic.

Empathy. That is key to interviewing suspects, particularly suspects in child cases. The crap you see on television, where the hot-shot detective yells at the suspect or throws him up against the wall and gets a confession is just that: crap.

Who wants to get yelled at? Think about it this way: as the investigator, you are trying to get a total stranger to admit to committing a crime that will put him in prison for the better part of the rest of their life. It's a very difficult job, and it takes a special kind of person who is willing to show empathy and listen to a monster who should never see the outside of a prison.

****

On April 17, 2012 at about 4:30 in the afternoon, a young mother named Megan[33] returned to the two-bedroom apartment she rented with her live-in boyfriend. The boyfriend's name was Carl David. He was twenty-four years old. They had been dating for about a year and moved into the apartment together in October. Megan had been out job hunting during the day while two of her three children were in school. The apartment was located on the south side of Fairbanks near 17th Avenue. The oldest of the three children was a six-year-old boy followed by a five-year-old girl. The youngest of the three was a little two-year-old boy named Kyle[34].

---

33 This name has been changed.
34 This name has been changed.

When Megan walked in the apartment, David was sitting on the living room couch holding Kyle's limp body in his arms. Blood was dripping from the two-year-old boy's mouth. David tried to explain to Megan that her six-year-old son had pooped in his pants and that Kyle tried to help the older boy clean himself. He grabbed Kyle and threw him on a bed. He claimed that Kyle bounced off the bed and hit the wall before landing hard on the floor.

Megan was scared and didn't know what to do. She scooped Kyle up, put him in a stroller and ran with him to the emergency room. Kyle was alive but not conscious. In the ensuing days she caught hell from family and friends alike, even from some law enforcement officers because she never called 9-1-1. I gave her the benefit of the doubt.

From the front door of the apartment you can see the hospital, so in reality Kyle would not have made it to the emergency room much quicker if he had gone by ambulance. The physicians in the emergency room stabilized Kyle and called the police. Patrol officers responded immediately. Some officers drove to the hospital while some went straight to the apartment to make contact with David. Photos were taken of Kyle's battered little body before he was flown to Providence Hospital in Anchorage. David was detained and brought to the police department while an officer remained on scene to secure the apartment.

Detective Chris Nolan and I were called in to work that afternoon to interview David. We were briefed on the known circumstances of the case, including what David had told Megan. Of course, we knew his explanation of what had happened was totally fabricated. Our experience told us the mechanism of injury he described could not have caused the injuries little Kyle had sustained. What caused those injuries was still a mystery, because we were waiting on a preliminary report from the emergency room physicians.

Chris and I found David in a holding cell on the first floor of the police department. We acted friendly and introduced ourselves before walking with him upstairs to an interview room in the investigations division. At this point, we needed to be David's friends. He needed to trust us and had to believe that, no matter what he told us, we would understand and help him through this difficult time. After all, we were fathers and understood how frustrating kids can be. Accidents happen right?

That is the mindset that the academy student who asked that question will never understand or be able to wrap his brain around. Before you talk to a guy like David, or any child predator, you have to tell yourself to stay calm and no matter what you cannot get frustrated. Do not get angry during the interview despite the God awful atrocities they have allegedly committed. If you get mad and start yelling, they won't talk. Who likes to talk to someone who is yelling at them? No one does unless you are on television. Only Hollywood detectives get confessions when they yell. There will be a time to be angry later but not now. You need the confession. Without any witnesses, we have to make this guy hang himself with his own words and let him put himself in jail for the rest of his miserable life.

Now, David sat facing the door. I wanted the camera looking him square in the face to capture his emotions, or lack thereof. I began, "David, whenever someone is brought down to the police station and put into handcuffs...well, I'm going to read you your rights, okay? That does not mean that you are under arrest at this time, and I want you to understand that. It's a formality because you have been handcuffed and put into a holding cell."

I pulled out my battered old Miranda card and read the same warning I had recited hundreds of times before. David verbally waived his rights and agreed to speak with us.

A light tapping on the interview room door caught my attention. "David, I need to step out for just a second."

Chris picked up the conversation with David where I left off. When I stepped out of the room, Lt. Welborn motioned for me to follow him into our office.

"I have an update on Kyle."

"Is he still alive?"

"Yeah, but he's being flown to Anchorage immediately. He has a huge crack in his skull and his neck is broken. He also had retinal hemorrhaging and severe bruising on his abdomen and groin. He is not expected to survive."

"On his groin? What do you mean?"

He handed me some photos that an officer in the emergency room had emailed him. "Here, look at these."

"Oh my God." I could feel the tears welling up in my eyes. I fought hard to hold them back. Kyle was covered from head-to-toe with fresh bruises. His cheeks were covered with elongated black-and-blue lines shaped like fingers. He had obviously been smacked in the face multiple times, and his abdomen was bruised, but the most shocking injuries that could be seen without an x-ray were on his groin. His entire groin area was mangled. His little penis and scrotum were different shades of purple, black, and blue. That photo shook me to the core. It took me a minute to catch my breath and regain my composure before I went back into the interview room.

Chris resumed the questioning when I entered. "Carl, what happened today?"

He collapsed in the chair and meekly said, "Well, he wet the bed and I got kind of angry. I kind of spanked him a little bit, and I threw him on the bed, and that's when he bounced off and slammed the side of his head."

"On the wall?" Chris asked.

"On the floor," David answered. "He bounced off the bed and hit his head on the floor."

We had David's initial story, regardless if it was the truth or not, and we knew it wasn't based on Kyle's injuries. When investigating child physical abuse cases, it is just as important to prove what did *not* happen as what actually happened. Sometimes we may never know exactly what happened, because if the suspect doesn't disclose everything he did to the child, we have to prove he or she is lying, and it can be impossible to find out what they won't tell us. The mechanism of injury the abuser first describes often could not have caused the injuries to the child. In most cases, and Kyle's case was proving to be no different, the suspect usually says the child fell off a couch or a bed or the child fell and hit his head on a toy. It's the same fabricated story over and over again, case after case. But it gave us information on what couldn't have happened and let us know the suspect was lying. That's why it was important to get David's initial admissions. We could use his story as a baseline during the rest of the interview.

David stated, "I was just watching a movie and figured I had better go check on him. I took him to the tub and washed him and took his underwear off and soaked them. Then I threw him on the bed." David also described that although Kyle was only two, they had been trying to potty train him because they couldn't afford to keep buying diapers.

Chris continued his questioning. "One thing about the bed, if you are standing there and you toss him on the bed...did he hit the wall?"

"He bounced toward the edge. He bounced off the corner and hit his head on the floor."

I asked, "How were you holding him when you threw him on the bed?"

"I had him by his arm and his leg, his right arm and his right leg."

"What was he wearing?" I asked.

David said, "He was naked, and I put underwear on him after that."

"Was he awake then?" Chris asked.

"Kind of, he was just breathing and laying there."

We slowly began to press David harder for details about what he had done to Kyle. Chris and I kept telling him that we both had children and knew how frustrating they could be, especially at such a young age. We could sympathize with him, because as fathers, we got upset with our children, and just like him, had lost our cool a time or two.

The strategy seemed to work and David began to open up a bit more. He told us that after he pulled Kyle from the bed, he made him sit on a potty seat in the bathroom. Then he put Kyle in the bathtub to wash him. He became increasingly frustrated, so he smacked Kyle with an open hand three or four times to the side of his face.

Chris asked, "Why did you hit him in the face? Because he had gone to the bathroom?"

He responded, "I was just so angry."

"What else happened with him physically?" I asked. "I know you smacked him a few times and threw him on the bed, but what else happened? I know you know what I'm talking about because he's got some other injuries...and I'm really sorry we have to talk about this but...everything is fine, he's being checked out at the hospital and he's going to be fine. But his other injuries need to be explained."

I never told David what injuries I was talking about because I wanted to hear it from him. He knew I was talking about the bruising on Kyle's crotch but I wanted to hear him say what he had done without me putting words in his mouth.

"When he was lying on the floor, I kind of put my foot on him, on his groin area."

"You put your foot on his groin area?"

David slowly continued, "I was using my heel and kind of pushing down."

"But when you're pushing down with your heel on his groin, you're pissed still right?"

David said, "Yes."

"How long do you think your foot was on his crotch?"

"I pushed down three or four times."

"What made you stop?" I asked him.

"He wasn't moving or anything, he was just lying there not moving but he was breathing. Megan didn't come for about an hour."

An hour. David sat there with that poor, unconscious child in his lap who was fighting for his life, and David did nothing because he was "too scared" to call 9-1-1, too scared to ask a neighbor for help, and too scared to take Kyle to the hospital.

We took David back to the apartment where we recorded him walking us through the scene while he described what he had done to Kyle. He showed us the bed Kyle had bounced off. The cluttered room had toys strewn about. All three kids shared the same bed. Chris and I measured the distance from the floor to the top of the mattress. The distance was one and a half feet. The carpet was in fairly good shape, but we cut out a square piece exposing the pad beneath. These items were kept as evidence.

We knew he was still lying about how Kyle's skull cracked. There was no way he could have bounced off the mattress and cracked his skull on the carpeted floor. I arrested David that night for Assault in the First Degree, knowing full well that, by the time the case was brought before the grand jury, the charge would be upgraded to murder.

My nearly two-year-old twins were in bed when I got home that night. I walked into their room and looked at them for several minutes. Finally, sensing they were being watched, they slowly opened their eyes. I hugged both of them really hard and told them how much I loved them.

"Daddy, you catch bad guy?" my son asked.

"Yeah, buddy, we caught a bad guy." I put them back into their toddler beds and kissed them both on the forehead before slowly backing out of the room.

I've never understood how someone could hurt a child. I was so pissed off about what that man had done. Kyle was only two years old. Heaven forbid he peed in the underwear he probably shouldn't have been wearing anyway. Being a father of four kids (now five), I know a thing or two about potty training and poopy diapers. The kids don't like pooping on themselves any more than you enjoy cleaning it up. It's not their fault.

The next day Chris and I went to the Fairbanks Correctional Center to conduct a follow-up interview with Carl David. Again, he agreed to speak with us. We cut right to the chase; there was no point in messing around. It was time to find out how David had cracked Kyle's skull.

It didn't take long for David to admit what he had really done to Kyle. He dropped him in the bathtub. After Kyle sat on the kid's potty in the bathroom, David picked him up and dropped him into the bathtub from about waist high. David is 5'11". On the way down, Kyle smacked the back of his head on the side of the tub, causing a 5 mm wide crack in his fragile skull.

I hope...no...I pray that when Kyle hit his head, he was knocked unconscious. I pray that he was asleep and didn't have to look into the eyes of a man he loved and trusted, who helped raise him, while that man stepped on and battered his little body as he wondered, "Why are you doing this to me?" I pray he was asleep and didn't feel any pain.

****

I was called in one night to assist the Alaska State Troopers on a child death. The AST investigator and I, who is still a great friend of mine, were in the Fairbanks Memorial Hospital Emergency Room examining the body of a young boy. His chest and back were covered with silver dollar sized burn marks. It turns out, his mother had burned him repeatedly with a blow torch. I'm not sure how the case turned out.

****

"9-1-1, do you need police, fire, or medical?" It was one of a dozen 9-1-1 calls that Kristi would answer on the evening of May 15, 2006.

The male caller responded, "I need to report a burglary. Someone kicked in my front door."

"No problem, sir, can you describe what was taken from the residence?"

He continued, "Well that's what is weird. They only took my computers. Even my TV is still here."

Kristi hesitated. "Sir, can I put you on hold for just one moment?" She chose another line and called me at home.

"Hey, where did you serve that child porn warrant this afternoon?"

"I can't remember the house number, but it was on Lakloey Drive in North Pole. The suspect wasn't home, so we kicked in the door."

Kristi chuckled. "I think your suspect is calling 9-1-1 to report a burglary."

"That's funny. Tell him there should be a copy of the search warrant on his couch. The house was a mess so he may not see it right away." She hung up and returned to the original call.

"Sir, are you still there?"

"Yes."

"Can you walk over to your couch and see if there is some paperwork there? It should be a copy of a search warrant because the Fairbanks Police, FBI, and ATF served a warrant today at your house for child porn."

His response was awesome. "Oh, okay, thanks." Click.

Bradly Swanson[35] had got himself into a bit of a pickle. Like most twisted people who somehow get turned on the watching the systematic rape of young children, Swanson turned to the internet to search for child pornography. He stumbled upon a website that advertised exclusive and private memberships for those willing to pay a fee. For just a few dollars you could receive a virtually unlimited supply of child pornography videos and photographs at your perverted fingertips. All you had to do was enter your credit card number.

Once he paid for his membership, Swanson was diverted to a different website and provided a password to access the webpage that actually offered the child porn downloads. From there he was able to download dozens of child pornography videos and still images and save them in various folders on his computer.

Of course, Swanson was not the only person to purchase a membership to this particular website. Federal law enforcement

---

35 This name has been changed.

officers paid for their membership using a federal credit card. Working in an undercover capacity, the officers established that the website indeed delivered on what they advertised. They discovered where the server, or storage unit, for the website was located. This is where the webmasters stored all of the membership, and more importantly, the credit card data from their subscribers. The server for this particular website was located in Colorado. Federal search warrants were obtained and raids were conducted, and all of the credit card data stored on the server was analyzed. The name listed on one of the credit card accounts was Bradly Swanson of North Pole, Alaska. It was a hard lesson learned for Swanson: all of those websites that post assurances that they do not store your credit card data actually do.

I knew Swanson rather well. He had been the swimming teacher at Lathrop High School when I attended. He also coached the diving team. I always thought he was a little strange. The girls in my class thought he was even stranger. Now I know why. When I analyzed the computers we seized from his house I found over 250 videos depicting very young, from toddler age on up, children engaged in various sexual acts with adults. Add to that several hundred still images, and Swanson found himself indicted for seventy-five felony counts for Possession of Child Pornography. He went to jail for a couple years—not nearly long enough in my opinion, but the state-imposed sentences for child pornography are fairly low when compared to the federal system. As a side note, a few years later his son was arrested and found guilty of sexually abusing a young boy.

Swanson exercised his right to remain silent and declined to be interviewed. His was my first child pornography case. Since then, I have sat down with numerous men who somehow got wrapped up in the twisted world of child pornography. Even after getting into their heads and finding out why they enjoy watching such filth I still don't "get it." And maybe I'm not supposed to get it, and that's a good thing. At this point in my career I'm content with a good confession THAT they did it. I'm way past caring WHY they did it.

Working child pornography cases is very time consuming, and you kill a lot of trees before you ever come close to making an arrest. There is a lot of paperwork involved. Often investigators must obtain initial search warrants to obtain the account information for suspects from internet service providers. Then another warrant is required to search the suspect's home if the account information you obtained from the provider is current and correct. In some jurisdictions you must obtain a third warrant to forensically analyze any of the computer equipment you seized during the execution of the warrant at the residence.

I don't know how many times I have come home blurry eyed after staring at a computer screen all day scanning through the most God-awful images and videos. It's something not many people talk about because no one wants to hear about it. "Hey, how was your day? Mine was horrible," is a question I got from friends all the time. "Oh, it was great, I got to watch seventy-five videos of a little four-year-old girl being raped over and over and then ejaculated on. How bad was your day again?" Usually my day trumps theirs every time. I'm lucky I have a wife who will listen to just how my day was and why I might have a hard time playing with my kids for a little while after I get home.

These cases get to you. The images burn holes in your brain and implant pictures you will never, ever be able to erase. It is a really crappy job, but someone has to do it. I have a tremendous amount of respect for the men and woman who do computer forensics work all the time. That is their day, every single day. At least my days are broken up working on other serious cases. Their days are not.

One of my pet peeves about these types of cases is when I hear people say, "Who cares about child porn because no one gets hurt?" Or "It's a victimless crime." Or my personal favorite: "I'm just watching it; I'm not actually doing it."

Bullshit.

If you think that no one is getting hurt, you are out of your mind.

Come to think of it, if you get off watching this crap, you ARE out of your mind.

It is simple supply and demand economics. If someone in Fairbanks, Alaska demands child pornography, someone somewhere in the world is going to supply it for them. Obviously, the supply part of that equation requires the involvement of a child. The child gets hurt. It's that simple.

The people who spend their spare time watching these sordid videos play a key role in the brutalization of children around the world. They are either too stupid to realize it, just don't care, or stick their head in the sand and pretend they don't know.

But holy hell is it fun to put them in jail.

****

With two large military bases near Fairbanks, we end up with a lot of young soldiers with a lot of time on their hands. In 2007 I arrested two soldiers from the same infantry unit on Fort Wainwright. They both lived in the same barracks and both had been downloading child pornography movies from a file sharing network. Cybercrimes detectives from the Anchorage Police Department monitored their activities, and before they knew it, I came knocking with search warrants in hand for their barracks. The cases were investigated just a couple months apart.

After I arrested the second soldier, I had a sit down with the unit commander, Captain Alexander. I told him flat out that he had a problem in his unit. I had just arrested two soldiers from his unit in the span of only a couple months for possessing and distributing child pornography. These guys were totally autonomous as well. The cases were unrelated. The captain literally shrugged me off and told me he didn't think there was a problem in his unit. The cases were isolated incidents and that he would deal with the problem.

I was never in the military. However, thanks to my family's connections and my growing up near two military bases, I'm neither stupid nor completely ignorant when it comes to the chain of command and moving up the ladder. All captains want to become majors. This guy didn't want a black mark on his record the next time he was up for promotion. I called my close friend and hunting partner Bob Montgomery, who at the time was working for the Attorney General's Office. He also happened to be a paralegal for the JAG office on Fort Wainwright during his time in the Army.

"Bob, can you believe this? I just arrested two guys in two months from this guy's unit for child porn and he could care less... doesn't think he has a problem in his unit. He totally blew me off."

Bob was surprised. "Really? Let me make a call, and why don't you come pick me up."

An hour later, I was sitting in the colonel's office on Fort Wainwright. It had only taken an hour and two phone calls from Bob to set up the meeting. Bob walked into the colonel's office like he still worked there and shook the man's hand and talked about the old days for few minutes. Then we got down to business.

The colonel addressed me. "Detective Merideth, what can I do for you?"

I have to admit, I was a bit intimidated. This colonel was one of the highest ranking officers in any branch of military service in the State of Alaska. "Well sir, in the last couple months I have arrested two guys from this particular unit for possessing and distributing child pornography. They even live in the same barracks a floor apart, and they were not working together on this deal. That is quite a coincidence and very disturbing."

His mouth dropped open and for a long moment he looked like a fish out of water. Then his training kicked in. "What can we do to stop this? To make sure this doesn't ever happen again."

"I had a meeting with the commanding officer this morning, Captain Alexander. I explained to him what was going on and why his guys had been arrested. I even offered to meet with his men to talk about what internet sites to stay away from, etc. Sir, he blew me off, couldn't care less, told me he didn't have a problem in his unit, and that he would handle it."

"No, Detective Merideth. *I* will handle it." That was all that needed to be said.

At 8:00 A.M. the next morning, my desk phone rang.

"Detective Merideth? This is Captain Alexander, we spoke yesterday."

My curiosity was piqued. "Hi, what can I do for you?"

"Well, sir, I have been doing some thinking, and you are right. I think there is a problem in my unit, and I'm going to do everything I can to see this kind of thing never happens again. Thank you for meeting with me and bringing this matter to my attention."

I wanted to say something like, "Yeah, no shit, I bet you do. How does it feel to get your ass reamed by a full-bird colonel?" But I restrained myself. I had realized it's about something much bigger than him. It's about protecting the children who are used for these things and not getting another dig in.

"Captain, if there is anything I can do to help, just let me know."

****

In the United States there are sixty-one Internet Crimes Against Children (ICAC) Task Forces comprised of 3,000 local and federal law enforcement and prosecuting agencies. These agencies are responsible for the pro- and re-active investigation and prosecution of crimes related to children through the internet.

The bread-and-butter cases for most of these agencies are cases regarding the possession and distribution of child pornography. In Alaska, most of the cases pass through the Anchorage Police Department Cyber Crimes Unit before being distributed to the agency with jurisdiction. If a suspect resides in or around the Fairbanks area the case comes to me as the local ICAC representative. Some cases are initiated locally, for instance when someone drops a computer off to have the virus demons exorcised, they were infected with from surfing too much internet porn. The computer technicians observe what looks like child pornography to them, so they call the police. Such was the case with a guy named Todd Godowski[36].

On May 10, 2014, Todd Godowski dropped his computer off to be repaired at a local computer sales and service shop. He reported he had been infected by the "FBI virus." This particular virus attaches to your hard drive while the user surfs what seems like harmless pornography websites. A pop-up screen warns the user his or her computer has been locked by the FBI but for a fee your computer will be miraculously cured of this disease. Godowski never paid any money to the advertisers, but he did decide to have his computer virus professionally removed. As the technicians were working on the hard drive they observed what they believed to be child pornography. They were correct in their assessment.

A patrol officer seized the computer from the shop and forwarded the case to me. I obtained a search warrant to examine the computer for the presence of any child pornography. I quickly previewed the hard drive and found exactly what the computer technicians had discovered. A more complete forensic exam would be performed later, but for now I wanted to interview the guy who dropped the computer off before he called the shop and asked why the repairs were taking so long.

On May 30, 2014, Detective Scott Adams and I drove to Godowski's residence in North Pole. The house was average size with a detached garage across the driveway. We approached the door

---

36 This name has been changed.

cautiously never knowing what to expect. A check through APSIN[37] had revealed that Godowski was seventy-five years old, but the fact that he was elderly didn't deter us from being careful. I didn't know how many people lived in the house, but hopefully we would be lucky enough to catch Godowski home alone. For some reason, these conversations seem to go better when the suspect's wife is not at home. We knocked on the door and caught the attention of a noisy dog. It sounded like an ankle biter.

The door opened. "Hi, are you Mr. Godowski?"

"That would be me."

"My name is Peyton Merideth, and I am a detective with the Fairbanks Police Department, and this is Detective Adams. Do you have just a second or did I catch you at a bad time?"

"No, I was just in here watching a movie." I was afraid to ask *what* movie he was watching. It wouldn't be the first time we caught a suspect "in the act."

"We just needed to chat for a few minutes. I'm one of the guys that works on computers for the city and well, sometimes issues come up with computers, people hacking into other people's systems and things like that and well, that's what I need to talk to you about. Do you have a few minutes to talk?"

"Yeah, come on in." He was home alone, so that was a good sign and he had invited us into his home, so there was no need to read him his Miranda Warning. We all took a seat in the living room and exchanged pleasantries about the cold spring we had endured in the Interior this year. It didn't take too long for me to get down to business.

Finally, I said, "Do you know what I need to speak with you about?"

"Probably about what is on my computer."

Well, that was easy. I didn't exactly have to pry that out of him.

"Alright, well what can you tell me about that?"

"Nothing; I look at porn." He went on to describe the type of computer virus he had contracted and the unsuccessful steps he had taken to get rid of it. By doing this, Godowski essentially admitted he knew his way around a computer, making it difficult for him to play dumb later.

---

37 APSIN – Alaska Public Safety Information Network

"Well, obviously you know why we are here. They were working on your computer and saw some pictures on there that they thought were questionable with some kids and stuff." I played it off and told Godowski I just needed to make sure that no local kids were being hurt and that I couldn't really care less about what was on his computer. "Those pictures of all the kids, are those just pictures from the internet?"

He nodded. "It's just what you can cull off the internet. I got involved in it when I worked out in the bush all the time, and I had my own laptop I would take me with me. I was looking at porn out there when one of these child websites popped up, and I was like, hey, okay. Yeah, I just uh, started looking it, and that was pretty much it. Beyond the computer, I'm not into kids. That's just what you can get off the internet by searching."

I knew that a lot of folks in the villages found illegal ways to keep themselves occupied, but that didn't excuse him then or now. "Have you ever talked to anybody about this, about why you like looking at pictures of kids?"

"I've never thought about it that way." He said it so matter of fact like, without a hint of giving the notion a second thought.

"How many pictures do you think you have saved off the internet over the years?"

"Maybe a thousand? My wife died six years ago. I suppose that since I have more time, I do it more than what I used to. But I never thought of it...it's kind of like masturbation. They told us when we were younger...when you ask a guy if he masturbates and he says no, you know he's lying, and I look at porn the same way. I don't want to go out and run with kids, none of that."

"You just like looking at pictures of them having sex on the net." I kept my tone carefully neutral, not even bothering to phrase it as a question.

"Yeah, all you do is log on and bang, it's right there, it's what you see, and I figure I'm not hurting anybody."

"Is that something you masturbate to while you are watching it?" It's a gross question to ask but if they give an affirmative answer it really makes the suspect look guilty.

"Sure! Not the kid stuff so much, that just gets you ready to go and then after that..." And with that Godowski made a sound with his tongue to demonstrate what it sounds like when he ejaculates. Thankfully his phone rang, and he got up to answer it.

I looked over at Detective Adams and whispered, "Uh, Scott, that was gross. Anything else we need from this guy or can we go?" He just shook his head. We both wanted to leave and wash our hands as quickly as possible.

Godowski was later sentenced to twenty months in federal prison, not a long sentence but the court took notice of his age and health concerns. I did not share that story because the circumstances in the case are unique, because really they are not. Well, besides the fact no one has ever described to me the sound they make when they ejaculate. That was the first and hopefully last time I have the pleasure of hearing that noise in that context.

No, this case stood out to me because Godowski had justified in his own mind that what he was doing was fine because he believed, "No one is getting hurt." He had also convinced himself that he was not into watching kids have sex with adults because he only checked that action out to get himself ready to enjoy adult pornography.

But there is no excuse. And there is no victimless crime of child pornography.

****

I just can't understand what goes through the minds of people who are into child pornography. As a detective you must play into that mindset and understand it as best you can in order to get the confession. You have to speak their language.

In 2013 I investigated three Fairbanks cases that were serious enough to be prosecuted at the federal level. One suspect's name was William Holeman[38].

Holeman, like many others I have investigated, was downloading child porn using a file sharing network. Most people use these programs to download regular Hollywood movies and such. For some, however, they provide a never-ending pipeline of child pornography videos. Cybercrimes detectives with the Anchorage Police Department had been gathering videos Holeman had collected through the file sharing program. They finally had enough probable cause to serve a warrant on Holeman's internet service provider which revealed his identity. His address came back to an apartment building on the south side of Fairbanks, so the case ended up on my desk.

---

38 This name has been changed.

I interviewed Holeman in his apartment with Investigator Avery Thompson[39]. He lived alone, and it was easy to tell why. Holeman was a total recluse and a computer enthusiast. His entire life revolved around getting up in the morning, drinking Mountain Dew and getting on the internet. He was really into sword fighting and anime cartoons. There were swords and anime posters hanging on his walls. The most bizarre thing in the apartment though was a wall of empty Mtn. Dew boxes that were stacked from floor to ceiling against one side of his bedroom.

During our interview, Holeman admitted to downloading tons of child pornography. At one point I turned on one of his monitors to photograph what was displayed on the screen before shutting the computer down. The file sharing program was running and downloading child porn—while we had been interviewing him! When I turned on the monitor he said, "Oh shit, I'm in a lot of trouble huh?"

"Yep, you are," were the words that came to mind.

When I examined his computers in my office, I determined that Holeman was really into bestiality, which is people having sex with animals. He had tons of bestiality videos and he wasn't into just one species either. For him it was either child porn or animals. It's like he got up in the morning and flipped a coin to determine his preferences for the day.

One day he called me. A date had been set for his case to go before the federal grand jury. He would be arrested in less than a month. Of course he didn't know that.

"Detective Merideth, this is William Holeman. I had a few questions. I figure for now I should pretty much forget about volunteering at the Big Brothers Big Sisters organization?"

I was utterly speechless, which is not the norm for me. The best I could come up with was, "Uhhhh....yeah? Umm...that is not what I expected you to ask. Were you in the process of volunteering for them?"

"I was debating on going in for an interview."

Holy crap. "Well...uh...I can't really tell you what to do and what not to do...but uh...no, I don't think it's a good idea that you volunteer for Big Brothers Big Sisters right now." I was dumbfounded. "Was that pretty much the only thing you had on your mind?"

39 Avery Thompson is a still a detective with FPD. He is perhaps the most talented forensic cell phone examiner in the State of Alaska.

"Well, No."

Oh great. What could top that?

"Would it be possible, considering how long this will take, is it possible, considering how long this is going to take maybe, once you are done investigating and confiscating from the first computer, could I get that returned while you continue on with the rest of the stuff?"

Goodness. "Sure, William, that is possible." I was lying through my teeth. The computer was evidence. Besides, by then he was going to be in jail, so he wouldn't need it anyway.

"If somehow I make it out of this with both my dignity and freedom intact, is there some sort of way I can have you guys bug any computer systems I have that would more readily alert you guys if this were to happen again?"

Seriously? This guy was facing federal prosecution, and all he wanted was his computer back and clearly he already knew he was going to re-offend.

I told him I didn't think that was the best thing to do and that he needed to get professional help. By now I had the attention of everyone else in the office.

"Do you think I can leave the state and go visit some friends in Montana?" he then asked.

I couldn't resist. "Well, William, do your friends live on a farm? Like, with animals?" I had to cover the phone because everyone was laughing so hard.

He didn't hesitate, "Well yes, they sure do."

Those poor, poor animals, I thought.

Though I didn't actually say that. Even I have limits.

CHAPTER 11
A FALLEN HERO

On October 16, 2016, Sgt. Allen David Brandt was shot several times while patrolling the streets of Fairbanks, Alaska. Allen was responding with several officers to a shots fired call downtown when he noticed someone walking westbound on 8th Avenue away from the area, just north of the Westmark Hotel. As he approached the person, Allen slowed down. The person pulled out a handgun and opened fire, striking Allen's vehicle several times. Allen was shot three times in the legs, once in the center of the chest, and some shrapnel entered his left eye. Allen returned fire but missed his assailant, who wrestled away Allen's gun as Allen lay helpless on the ground. The suspect stole Allen's patrol vehicle and sped away while Allen called for help on his personal radio.

Allen was left for dead in a dark, vacant lot so the responding officers had a hard time finding him. He continued to shout directions over the radio, but officers kept driving by him. Finally, a wonderful lady who lived across the street, who was awakened by the sounds of the gunshots, ran to Allen's aide and called 9-1-1. Officers flooded the area and put a tourniquet on Allen's leg to try to stop the bleeding. Paramedics finally arrived and Allen was rushed to the Fairbanks Memorial Hospital.

Allen's patrol vehicle was found abandoned a short distance away between 8th and 9th Avenues along the Steese Highway. The suspect's gun and Allen's gun were found inside the vehicle, but the suspect was nowhere to be found. Officers from all surrounding law enforcement agencies began searching on foot and by vehicle, stopping every person and car coming and going from downtown Fairbanks.

A ringing cell phone on my nightstand woke me from a deep sleep. When I saw the private number flashing, I didn't think much of it; I was used to being wakened in the middle of the night by a dispatcher or a patrol supervisor telling me to get to work. I answered the phone in my usual groggy voice.

The dispatcher said, "S2 has been shot, you need to come to work."

I remember thinking, *who the hell is S2?* "Say that one more time."

"S2 has been shot, you need to come work."

"Okay, slow down. Is he alive?"

"He's at the hospital."

By this time my wife was awake and getting dressed. She knew that dispatch would be busy, so she was heading to work to help out.

As I got dressed I called my lieutenant and either texted or called the rest of our unit. All I know is, I was out of the house in five minutes and was speeding toward the hospital. When I got there, Allen was being treated in the emergency room by a team of doctors and nurses. He had a large bandage on his eye. The tourniquet was still wrapped around his leg stopping any possible arterial bleeding.

I held his hand and we prayed together. We talked about what had happened and what the suspect looked like so I could get the description out on the radio. Finally, they rolled Allen in for a CT scan to check for any serious internal bleeding before they removed the tourniquet. Allen's wife and his best friend arrived, so I took off to help my team search for the suspect.

Allen was flown to Anchorage that night where a team of doctors specializing in eye trauma, operated on Allen in an attempt to save the vision in his left eye. A few days later, still blind in his left eye, he flew home to recuperate.

On October 24, 2016, Allen walked into a Fairbanks City Council meeting addressed the council and the crowd in attendance. The words he spoke that night are etched on a plaque on the wall of honor in the Fairbanks Police Department.

"I am humbled by the honor, and I'm no exception to the rule. We have many fine officers that are far greater and have done better things than I have. I do appreciate the community support, and I know sometimes it's hard for officers to see whether or not the city supports us, but I've always said that by and large, the city does support its police officers and we're never going to have the support of the criminals and the anarchists, and to tell you the truth, they don't have my support either. However, I do support their constitutional rights and their free exercise of them. I've seen the hand of the Lord in my situation. Can you believe I was shot five times to the legs and I walked into this room? It's almost healed up, but right here over my heart where I wear my vest certainly saved my life there. I appreciate the support of the community and the Fairbanks Police Department, and the Anchorage Police Department, and the Alaska State Troopers and other officers. In fact, my kids have been, they really feel like this has been a great time because my best friend Phil McBroom out at North Pole Police Department, he's been watching my four kids with his four kids. Bless his wife's heart. They're watching eight kids. And the officers from the Anchorage Police Department and locally here have been providing them meals, and they really appreciate it, but our officers do a very hard job, and they need your support. Unfortunately, when an officer gets shot or something bad happens, it's just human nature. We don't think about things that we need until something bad happens. I don't blame anyone for that, but think about our officers. I've worked for the city for 12 years. Probably 10 of those years I work weekends when my friends are off. I work at night and sleep during the day, don't sleep with my wife. And the other officers, too. I was never called a racist until I put the uniform on. Once you put a police uniform on, you're racist. I can't ever let my guard down, not at Fred Meyer and out of my house. I travel everywhere armed, always vigilant, always watching, and the other officers over there, they're the same way. So we need your support, not just when bad things happen, but the officers over there do a hard job and most of the time it's thankless, and we really appreciated *the outpouring of support that's come from this, and I think Sergeant Barnett's here. I want to thank him, Officer Phil McBroom and Sergeant Barnett. Sergeant Barnett was the first one on scene and until he got that tourniquet on my leg, I didn't think I was going to survive, because I was bleeding a lot. But let me leave you with this last story. The night that I was shot, I had my four kids and my wife on my bed, and I read them a story like I do - and after the story I told them, "I think I'm going to get shot tonight," and I'm in the middle of a gun battle, that's all I could think about and the first two people to call her to tell her, she hung up on because she thought I was playing a practical joke on her, and she thought it was a cruel joke. I wouldn't have done that to her, but can you imagine telling your kids before you go to work that you're going to get shot? Well, that's what our police officers deal with every day, and I'm not complaining, but I just want you to know what it's like in the life of a police officer, but we appreciate your support."*

On October 27, 2016, Allen returned to Anchorage for follow-up surgery to try and repair the vision in his left eye.

On October 28, 2016, Allen died in Anchorage from surgery complications. The cause of death was blood clots in his lungs, but the manner of death was homicide. I remember getting the call, this time from my wife, that Allen's heart had stopped beating several times and the situation was not good. I also remember the call I got later that day from another detective telling me that Allen had died. I will never forget those calls and I will never forget holding my friend's hand in the hospital as we prayed together.

Allen was shot by a man named Anthony Jenkins. Prior to ambushing Allen inside his patrol vehicle, Jenkins walked out of his girlfriend's house on 9th Avenue, looked to the west and fired several shots at the Westmark Hotel. He was intoxicated and disgruntled because about a year earlier, a Fairbanks Police Department officer shot and killed one of his friends during a botched robbery. The shooting was clearly justified. Whether Jenkins fired those shots into the hotel to lure an officer to an ambush is debatable, but that was the result.

After shooting Allen and stealing his cruiser, Jenkins abandoned the vehicle in front of an auto repair shop along the Steese Highway between 8th and 9th Avenues. He can be seen on footage captured on the in-dash camera in the patrol vehicle walking calmly away as if nothing happened. He made his way down the street and ditched his clothes behind a friend's house on 9th Avenue.

In the hours following the shooting, the entire department worked tirelessly to find the shooter while still responding to emergency calls around the city. Our investigations unit followed up on every lead and phone call until we finally got a hot tip. A couple hours before the shooting, a guy walking under a bridge along the Chena River ran into Jenkins and a couple friends. For some reason, most likely because he was drunk, Jenkins confronted the guy and identified himself as, "Antman." We searched a database using the moniker "Antman." We immediately got a hit on his real name. Through social media, we discovered his girlfriend lived on 9th Avenue down the street from the Westmark Hotel. More importantly, police had discovered several spent shell casings on the street in front of the girlfriend's house. Presumably, these were the spent casings from the bullets that had been shot into the Westmark Hotel.

The Statewide Drug Enforcement Unit rented a room on the east side of the Westmark Hotel and set up surveillance on the girlfriend's house. I obtained search warrants for her house and the house across the street where Scott Adams had found Jenkin's clothes stashed in a shed in the backyard. FPD and AST SWAT teams were on standby to simultaneously hit both houses to look for Jenkins and evidence.

In the early morning hours of the 18th, about three hours before the planned raid on both houses, our surveillance team watched a subject matching Jenkins's description slip out of the house and walk East on 9th Avenue. I was in the station with our Chief, making final alterations to our operations plan when he heard the radio traffic about Jenkins leaving the house. We ran from the office, jumped in our cars, and headed that way. One of our patrol officers contacted Jenkins on the south bank of Chena River near the Clay Street Cemetery. He surrendered without a fight and was taken into custody without incident.

While SWAT operators and detectives seized and searched the two houses, Detective Avery Thompson and I interviewed Jenkins at FPD. He waived his Miranda rights and denied any involvement in the shooting. This cat-and-mouse game played out for a while until we got our lucky break. Detectives searching his girlfriend's home discovered some letters inside a pair of pants that belonged to Jenkins. One was an apology letter, written to Allen and his family explaining why he had shot him.

The rest of the case came together quickly. During a long and detailed confession, Jenkins confessed to the shooting. Blood found on the clothing found stashed near the scene belonged to Allen, and ballistic testing matched the gun left behind in Allen's vehicle to spent casings found at the scene.

I was so proud of the way our investigations team and the rest of the Fairbanks Police Department came together to support one another during that difficult time. Allen's family, his wife and four children, became our family. We held a united front committed to justice for Allen through the investigation and later during the long, difficult trial. Jenkins was found guilty of Murder in the First Degree and other related felony charges. He will spend the rest of his miserable life in prison.

CHAPTER 12
A BIG BULL FOR ALLEN

As I've mentioned before, hunting and spending time in the outdoors with friends and family is my passion. So many hunters in the Lower 48 dream of going on just one hunting trip in Alaska. I have been so lucky to have hunted all over the state and have shared so many wonderful experiences with friends and family.

In February 2017, four months after Allen's death, I dedicated a special hunt on Nunivak Island in western Alaska to Allen. We had talked about hunting muskox a lot and Allen was really excited, and a tad bit jealous I had drawn the tag in the state lottery. The following manuscript was printed in the January 2018 issue of Bowhunter Magazine. With their permission and support, I have included the story in this book.

****

I had to find the arrow. The cold arctic wind was pounding my face, and the snow was blowing in my eyes as I scanned the trampled path left by the herd as it thundered away. Dustin, my close friend and hunting partner, was filming the action from nearly 200 yards away and had no idea what I was doing. Then it dawned on him—Peyton was looking for his arrow.

As if it was dropped from the sky, I found my arrow sunken in two inches of snow next to the trampled trail. This arrow was special. Special because inked on each fletching was the number 202–badge number 202–worn by my friend and avid bowhunter Sergeant Allen Brandt who was killed in the line of duty on October 28, 2016.

I had been a police officer for eighteen years and losing a brother and then investigating his murder was easily the most painful and stressful experience of my career, and one I pray I will never again endure. In keeping with law enforcement tradition, a vigil was held over Allen's body at the funeral home in the days leading up to the service. Twenty four hours a day officers stood next to the body of our friend and brother. Next to the flag-draped casket was a table with a photo of Allen with a grizzly bear he had killed with his bow a few years back. Next to the picture I placed an arrow with the number 202 on the fletching. I was going to shoot a muskox in honor of my friend and I was going to do it with that arrow.

The rocky shore of Nunivak Island lies thirty miles off the coast of western Alaska in the Bering Sea. The only village there is Mekoryuk, which was home to about 200 Cup'ig Eskimos. Between and 1935 and 1936, the State of Alaska transplanted thirty-one muskoxen from Greenland to Nunivak hoping to establish a herd large enough to provide hunting opportunities for the Cup'ig people. The herd flourished, and muskoxen from this herd have been successfully transplanted to other regions in northern Alaska. In recent years, the Department of Fish and Game has rewarded between ten and forty bull tags during the annual tag lottery. Still, the odds of drawing a Nunivak Island tag are less than 5%. After years of applying, 2016 was our lucky year as Dustin Etchison and I both drew permits for the February 2017 hunt. We immediately began preparing and booked the services of registered guide and transporter James Whitman. Then in October my world was devasted when fellow police officer and bowhunter Allen Brandt was murdered in the line of duty in Fairbanks. Through dealing with the loss of Allen, it became clear that my muskox hunt would take on very special meaning.

As with any arctic hunt, the importance of planning and gear selection is paramount due to the harshness of the environment. This harshness is intensified when you factor in that you are hunting on an island in the middle of the Bering Sea, in the middle of the Alaskan winter. Just flying to the island is a challenge. Dustin and I endured ten hours of boredom in a small airport terminal in Bethel while two flights to Mekoryuk were cancelled in one day due to a low ceiling and drifting snow at the airstrip in Mekoryuk. On February 7, the weather broke over the island and our Cessna Caravan flew over the Yukon-Kuskokwim Delta and then over Nelson Island. As I looked down on the arctic moonscape, I was reminded of how fortunate I was to be alive and experiencing such an incredible adventure.

We were met at the airstrip by James and his assistant guide Raymond Amos. Ray was our official transporter for the hunt, and he wasted no time packing our gear into two sleds. The weather was good, so we were going hunting immediately. We raced by snow machines to James' house, changed into our hunting and cold weather gear and hit the trail. Hunting the same day you are airborne is illegal in Alaska, unless the flight is a regularly scheduled commercial flight. Our flight fell into that category, so it was legal to hunt the same day we flew to Mekoryuk.

Hunting, and really all activities on Nunivak Island, revolve around the weather. Nunivak's beautiful and exotic snowbound landscape can be deceiving and dangerous. The farther away from Mekoryuk you travel by snow machine, the farther you are from any type of civilization or shelter. We traveled south along the Mekoryuk River for a couple of miles, and then headed overland across the tundra. Our destination was a mountain about ten miles from the village that would be a good spot from which to glass the terrain for muskox. When we stopped after about six miles to take a quick break, we noticed a large herd of muskox on top of the mountain where we were headed! The muskox looked like a line of little black dots stretched over the top of the distant peak.

We closed the four mile gap quickly and parked our machines at the base of the mountain, which in reality is a very deceiving 800 feet in elevation. The herd of muskox peered down over the peak at us as we began our slow march up the slope. Every step was a struggle as our boots sank through the snow. Halfway up we were getting overheated, so we shed our parkas. Dustin was up first, so our plan was to go our separate ways and approach the herd on both sides in hopes they would form a defensive circle and not run away from us down the backside of the mountain. The plan was not working, and the herd was paying attention to me, until Dustin popped over the ridge. The herd spooked and ran straight away from us down the backside of the mountain. I crested the top and found the torn up swath of snow and ground left by the herd as they fled.

I followed the trail and worked my way down the back side of the mountain until the herd came into view. There was Dustin, moving in on a group of three bulls that had separated themselves from the main herd. I started filming him just as he drew his bow and shot one of the large bulls. The entire herd stampeded down the hill, but the wounded bull lagged behind. Soon, the two other bulls joined the bull that Dustin had shot, and the three stopped running and turned to face their assailant. Dustin worked his way closer and put a finishing arrow into the bull's vitals, and the big animal was down in seconds. I was ecstatic for my friend. We had landed on the island just two hours ago!

We spent the next couple of hours caping (taking the hide off) and butchering the bull. Ray gave us direction as needed, but as a contracted transporter he is not allowed to help with the butchering in the field. I am sure he got frustrated watching us make mistakes as we fumbled through the bull's long hair, but we got it done before dark and arrived back in Mekoryuk just as dinner was being served.

Ominous dark skies and a brisk wind blowing fresh snow greeted us the next morning. I was worried we were not going to make it out, but after breakfast Ray told us he wanted to at least try to find the same herd from the day before. There was one other big bull in the herd, and Ray felt they would seek safety on top of the mountain and stay there. We took the same route along the Mekoryuk River, but the conditions were terrible. It was as close to a total whiteout as I've ever encountered, and the flat light conditions made driving the snow machines very difficult. At any time I was expecting Ray to turn around and head home, but we pressed on. After an hour we started working what I believed to be uphill, but it was so nasty it was difficult to tell. We stopped in a low saddle just below the crest of the mountain where we had left the herd the day before. Sure enough, through the blowing snow I could make out the long line of muskox standing on top of the ridge. The conditions were too treacherous to hunt elsewhere, so we were either hunting this herd all day, or returning to the safety of Mekoryuk. We pressed on.

Dustin and I left Ray and the sleds and headed up the ridge. Once again, we separated to work the herd from both sides. When I got within about 100 yards, the herd took off and ran down the backside of the ridge, all the way to the bottom. We gave chase until they disappeared over a far ridge. I lost sight of Dustin who was below me a couple hundred yards, so I decided to walk back uphill toward Ray and the sleds. When I crested the top of the ridge, I ran into the herd. Evidently, they had circled around and gone back up the hill where they ran into Ray who was drinking coffee!

I turned on the GoPro mounted on the front of my bow and slowly began working toward the herd. They bunched up and formed a sort of shifting undulating circle that never stopped moving. From what I could tell, the largest bull in the herd was standing broadside at about 25 yards but there were too many animals behind him to shoot. When he finally shifted clear, I took one last reading with my rangefinder.

My release (a mechanical release to pull the string back) was frozen! I couldn't believe it. I started blowing warm air into my hand and worked the trigger back and forth until it was movable. I finally got the release on my bow string, and was drawing as the herd bounded away down the hill. Nearly two hours had passed, and I admit I was getting pretty frustrated. Dustin calmed me down a bit and convinced me everything would work out.

We jumped on the snow machines and drove around the North side of the mountain, which flanks the Mekoryuk River. On the flat river bottom, the herd had separated into several smaller groups. As we approached, one group ran right back up the mountain, but a smaller group of about twenty or so animals stayed down in the bottom. As required by law, Ray stayed behind while Dustin and I drove around the herd and stopped a couple yards away. There was no way of knowing if the big bull was in the group I was stalking, or with the part of the herd that had retreated uphill. I worked to within forty yards and they ran off. I was exhausted by this point, and was secretly wishing I had brought my muzzle loader. The herd stopped and formed a shifting circle a couple hundred yards from me. This time I nocked my 202 arrow, said a little prayer, and started moving toward the herd. At forty yards, the herd stayed put. Maybe it would this time?

Curiously, the wind died and the blowing snow subsided. I would have been totally content with a thirty yard shot, but all the animals on my side of the herd were cows and illegal to hunt. At twenty-five yards, the herd shifted again, and the big bull turned away from the center of the herd and faced me. I took three steps closer. I had been blowing on my release held in my cupped bare hand, so it attached easily onto the string. The bull stepped into the clear and I drew and released. The 202 arrow penetrated perfectly into the bull's chest cavity. He bounded away and piled up within 30 seconds.

I heard Ray screaming something, and then I heard Dustin screaming, "Way to go, Peyton!" While they were screaming I was crying. It was an emotional moment. I had embarked on an adventure, a difficult hunt to an island in the Bering Sea in the dead of winter. I had promised myself that I would kill a muskox in honor of my fallen brother, and I had succeeded. I had to find the arrow and I did. It was bloody and broken by the powerful movement of the bull's shoulder on his death run, but the 202 inked on the fletching had not been rubbed away.

The bull was a massive old warrior. James told me later that night that he was biggest bull killed so far during the short season. I couldn't have been more proud as I wrapped my hands around his long curling horns and ran my fingers through the hair along his back. What an awesome animal and fitting tribute to my friend.

EPILOGUE

Shortly before his death, Allen gave his son a .357 lever action rifle. It was built for a child, with a short stock and the light recoil was perfect for a nine year old boy who wanted nothing more than to follow his dad into the woods and maybe, just maybe, get a shot at an unsuspecting critter that he could bring home to show his mom. He reminded me of myself when I was nine. I had gotten a .22 Chipmunk rifle for Christmas. A couple of days later and full of anticipation for my first big hunt, I followed my dad into the woods, trudging through knee deep snow looking for an unsuspecting grouse. After what seemed like hours, my dad spotted a lone spruce grouse perched in a tree. My dad knelt down, and I rested the rifle over his shoulder for support. Even with a steady rest, the crosshairs in my scope danced all over the bird. I tried to calm my nerves and slow my breathing as I squeezed the trigger. The bird fell to the ground. It was a perfect day.

Allen's son will never get the chance to make wonderful memories hunting with his dad. He won't get the chance because his dad was stolen from him by a coward. On January 28, 2020, Anthony Jenkins was sentenced to 119 years in prison for murdering Allen. At the sentencing, Allen's brother testified on behalf of Allen's family. I was honored to speak on behalf of the Fairbanks law enforcement community. It was very difficult to get up in front of my friends, family and brothers and sisters in blue and recite words that reflect not only how I felt about Jenkins but also what they wanted to say. It was tough and emotional. Allen's brother was very eloquent and summed up his thoughts with:

"Allen was confident in his faith and those who knew Allen will be assured of where Allen will spend eternity. As for an earthly penalty for your crimes Mr. Jenkins, if 119 years is a high penalty, there cannot be too great a penalty for destroying such a great star as Allen Brandt,"

I would be remiss if I did not mention two other friends who gave up their lives, serving the citizens of the State of Alaska. Alaska State Troopers Sgt. Scott Johnson and Trooper Gabe Rich were shot and killed serving an arrest warrant in the village of Tanana, Alaska on May 1, 2014. Gabe was a local kid from Fairbanks and was loved by all. He left behind his fiancée , and new baby boy. Gabe was a student in some of my academy classes and I remember him as the kind of police officer I would want to respond to my house if my wife called 911 and needed help[40].

Scott Johnson was a friend and mentor. It literally crushed me when he died. My wife held me in her arms while I cried my eyes out. I looked up to Scott, as did so many law enforcement officers across the State of Alaska throughout his 20 plus year career. He was an outstanding Trooper, hunter, father and husband. I look back fondly over all the poker games and beers we shared together.

As for me, I retired as a patrol lieutenant in December of 2020 and moved south to the area around Boise, Idaho. The Treasure Valley, as it's called, is beautiful and the weather is fantastic. I spent a lifetime dealing with the long, cold brutal Fairbanks winters. Now I play golf year-round, which suits me fine and the hunting and fishing isn't bad either. Still though, the transition was very hard on me. I miss the job and the people I worked with in Fairbanks. I miss the uniform and the respect it carries. I miss the camaraderie and the sense of belonging. But it was my time to go.

I found a new home, supervising the Investigations Division with the Ada County Prosecutor's Office in Boise, ID. I'm not accustomed to working in an office with 180 people, but I adjusted quickly mostly because my superiors have been totally supportive of me since I was hired. The work isn't traditional police work, but that's ok because I spent a lifetime experiencing the worst society could dish out and it prepared me for my new career.

I'm ready for the next chapter of my life to begin.

---

40 On November 3, 2016, Nathaniel Kangas was sentenced to 203 years in prison for the murder of Troopers Scott Johnson and Gabe Rich.

Always remember that there are men and woman, risking their lives night and day to protect society. These heroes are the front line and the stewards of our freedom. Too often they are taken for granted until they are gone. Never forget those who have sacrificed their lives for the good of the many.

It was difficult deciding which cases and events to highlight in this book. I had so many adventures throughout my career, so many that I could ramble on for pages and bore even the most dedicated true crime fan. I chose these cases because they represent an overall sampling of what life is like for a police officer in interior Alaska. I hope you enjoyed my stories.

ACKNOWLEDGMENTS

The stories in this book are true. I don't believe I could write a real true crime memoir without being brutally honest and telling my readers exactly what happened as it happened. While Fairbanks and the surrounding Tanana Valley are wonderful places to raise a family there is also an undercurrent of crime flowing as swiftly and as surely as the Chena River flows through downtown. These stories are mine and I believe they should be told.

I have worked with so many talented and dedicated law enforcement officers and support staff over the years that it is difficult to thank everyone who in some special way made writing this book a reality. The families of so many victims have touched my soul during my career.

I would be remiss if I did not single out a few people who have helped me along the path making this book possible. To my editor, Kelsie Stone, thank you for your patience and hard work making my cop style of writing bearable for someone other than a cop to read. Now, if you could only teach me how to drink whiskey.

To my beautiful wife, soul mate and best friend Kristi, thank you for your tireless support throughout this project and my career. Thank you for always listening to the horrible stories I bring home, for wiping my tears and celebrating my successes. There is no one on earth I would rather have made this long journey with.

To the detectives and officers I have had the pleasure of working with over the years, thank you for helping me do my job better. We made one hell of a team. I realize that I have not mentioned every officer I worked with and for that, I am sorry but there are just too many to list.

To my readers, some of these stories are funny and writing about them made me smile and think fondly of fun times on the job. Others still make the hair on the back of my neck stand up or bring a tear to my eye. The experiences behind these stories molded me into the police officer I have become and made me the person I am. I hope you enjoyed them.

ABOUT THE AUTHOR

Peyton Merideth was born in Memphis, Tennessee in 1977. When he was just four years old, his parents uprooted and moved to Fairbanks, AK where they enjoyed long careers with the North Star Borough School District. Peyton attended Nordale Elementary, Tanana Jr. High, and graduated from Lathrop High School in 1995. It was during his sophomore year at the University of Alaska Fairbanks that he decided on a career in public service. He enrolled in the Interior Alaska Police Academy in 1998, the same year he obtained his B.A. in criminal justice. He also holds a M.A. in justice administration from the University of Alaska.

After college Peyton became a reserve officer for the City of North Pole. Not long after he was offered a full-time job as a police officer with the North Pole Police Department. After a year, and eager for the fast-paced action in a larger department, Peyton was hired as a police officer in Fairbanks. He spent the next five years answering hundreds of 9-1-1 calls and investigated a variety of crimes including assaults, thefts and motor vehicle accidents. His time in patrol provided a strong foundation for the next chapter of his career in investigations.

In 2005, Peyton was promoted to detective where for thirteen years he served the citizens of Fairbanks investigating brutal homicides, general death cases, sexual assault, child sexual abuse, child pornography cases, and officer involved shootings. In 2018, he was promoted to Sergeant and returned to patrol as a shift supervisor. He retired as a lieutenant in 2020 and moved to Boise, Idaho to be closer to his older children attending college. He has continued his career in Boise as the supervisor of the Investigations Unit with the Ada County Prosecutor's Office.

Peyton spends his leisure time with his family or hunting. His passion is hunting in Southern Africa where he claims you cannot get any farther from the streets of Fairbanks, AK without getting closer again. He is married to Kristi and the father of five children, three handsome sons and two beautiful daughters.

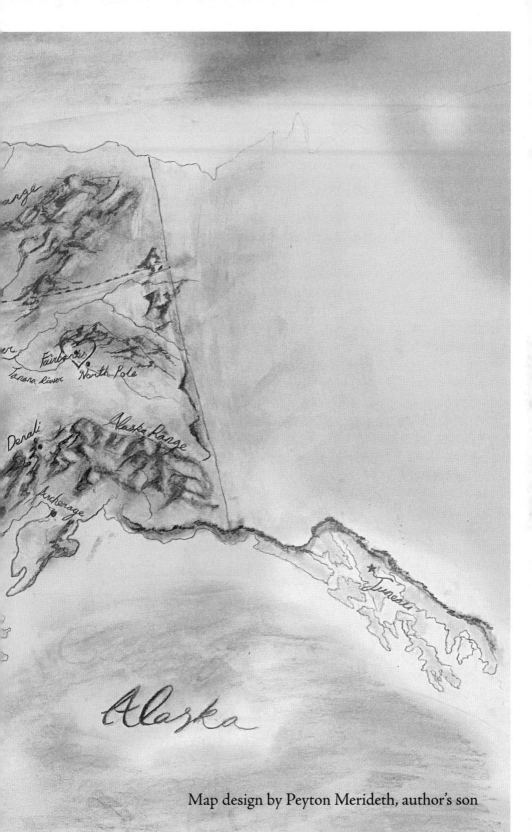

Map design by Peyton Merideth, author's son